THERE ARE MANY PEOPLE to whom I am forever grateful for their help and support while I went through the process of writing a second book. First, to Aysha and Alex, my amazing children. Your love, patience, understanding and help in keeping our house from looking like a tornado went through it are greatly appreciated. I love you guys. To my parents, who have always given me unconditional love and support in all that I do. I love you both. To my friends who have once again put up with my being absent for the past six months while I wrote this book. I am lucky to have you all in my life. To MaryJo Regier and Jodi Amidei for all of your help brainstorming and getting this book off the ground and through the proposal stages. You are amazing inspirations to me. To my editor, Amy Glander, for all of your help and advice while I was writing this book. I am grateful to have been able to work with you again. You are the best! And finally to Memory Makers Books for once again giving me this amazing opportunity. I will be forever grateful.

table of contents

Introduction 6

Textiles 8-27
Sewing Notions 10
Fabric 12
Lace 14
Ribbon 16
Machine Sewing 18
Embroidery 20
Hand Sewing 22
Silk Flowers 24
Fibers 26

CHAPTER **1** **TEXTILES**

Metals 28-45
Wire 30
Wire Mesh 32
Hardware 34
Embossing Metal 36
Metal Moldings 38
Metal Letters and Words 40
Charms 42
Brads and Eyelets 44

CHAPTER **2** **METALS**

Natural Elements 46-63
Flowers and Leaves 48
Mica 50
Burlap 52
Cork 54
Wood 56
Sandpaper 58
Hemp Twine and Twill 60
Marauyma Mesh 62

CHAPTER **3** **NATURAL ELEMENTS**

Art Mediums 64-83
Crackle 66
Texture Paste 68
Air-Dry Clay 70
Transfer Ink 72
Paper Perfect 74
Alcohol Inks 76
Metallic Flakes 78
Batik Resist Medium 80
Adirondack Wash 82

CHAPTER 4 ART MEDIUMS

Paper 84-103
Patterned Paper 86
Handmade Paper 88
Watercolor Paper 90
Paper Piercing 92
Dry Embossing 94
Chipboard 96
Cardboard 98
Puffy Paper 100
Distressing 102

CHAPTER 5 PAPER

Clear Elements 104-117
Beads 106
Sequins 108
Transparencies 110
Acrylics 112
Shrink Plastic 114
Glass 116

CHAPTER 6 CLEAR ELEMENTS

Supply Lists 118
Source Guide 124
About the Author 126
Index 127

If there is one thing that is evident it's that Alex loves the beach, so he is always excited for when Dean has his annual "Sawyer's Family BBQ". The BBQ is always at Dean's house , which is right on the beach so it means an afternoon playing in the sand, riding his boat out to check the crab traps (with a detour around the bay) and jumping on the trampoline, plus there are always tons of other kids there for him to play with. This time they also had big bubble wands for the kids to play with so after dinner, once the younger kids were getting tired and the bubble wands were free, Alex managed to sneak down on the beach and have a go with them. As a breeze was blowing in just the right direction, he was trying to aim them just right so that they would pop on his grandpa's head as he was sat on a chair chatting to the other guests. Ah, to be a kid again!

7/09/06

ON THE BEACH

ALEX

WHILE NEARING THE COMPLETION of my first book, *Embellished Emotions for Scrapbookers*, I knew I was going to have empty nest syndrome when the time came to tape up my last box of artwork and hand it over to the UPS guy. So I contacted my editors at Memory Makers Books and threw some new book ideas their way. Understandably, they laughed since I hadn't completed the first one yet, but replied saying they had a book idea they thought I would be perfect for—a book on textures. So the wheels in my brain started spinning and *Tantalizing Textures* was born.

Those who know me know I never started scrapbooking to have my photos in an archival-safe environment (that was just an added bonus). I started because I wanted a creative outlet that combined photographs and memories of my family and friends. Having been an artist all my life, I did not think I should be limited to what I put on my pages. So I allowed my creativity to take over and the page design to naturally evolve, and the result was highly textural pages that just begged to be touched.

But through my journey, I discovered that not all textures are thick and lumpy or even touchable. There are many different forms of texture and some of these are visual. Our photos are naturally filled this visual texture from the various settings we shoot in: a sandy beach, the trees in the back yard or the brick fireplace in the living room. As you'll see on the pages that follow, these visual textures create different moods that can be fun and inspiring to relay through *real* texture on your pages. You will also see how the form of texture you choose to include can be inspired by the subject itself, such as a youthful child, a pet's fur or a flower's delicate petals. The key is to allow textural design to enhance, not overwhelm, your photographs. This is not always an easy balance, but one I promise you'll soon feel comfortable achieving.

So please join me on this journey as we explore the tantalizing world of texture. You'll discover a wealth of inspiring ideas for adding a new depth and richness to your scrapbook art in ways you never thought possible.

Trudy

Trudy Sigurdson
Author and Artist
Tantalizing Textures

MONSTER MOGS

Who says our family members should only have 2 legs?

At 6 years old.

Not me. Every family needs a hairy member like our Monster Mogs.

7/16/06

The *bond* that links your true *family* is not one of blood, but of *respect* and *joy* in each other's life. -Richard Bach

textiles 1

Sewing Notions

Fabric

Lace

Ribbon

Machine Sewing

Embroidery

Hand Sewing

Silk Flowers

Fibers

TEXTILES ARE ONE OF the first types of textures we are exposed to. In infancy we are tightly swaddled with a soft cotton blanket to comfort and soothe us. As adults we unknowingly think about textiles as we decide between the soft and fluffy knitted sweater or the thick and chunky one. We contemplate if our window coverings match our sofa and how we can pull in a contrasting texture through the fabric on the cushions. So with many of us making these decisions in our everyday lives, why not apply these same thoughts and choices to our scrapbook pages?

Textiles cover a wide array of items and are a great introductory way for you to start incorporating texture onto your scrapbook pages. Plus, they are inexpensive and readily available…you probably already have many of these items in your home just waiting to be used. Learn how to use a simple textile such as ribbon to add texture in the traditional flat way, or spice it up by adding dimension. Or, discover how the different textures of the fabrics you choose can alter the mood of a page. Discover some unique and fun ways to experiment with the variety of textiles in the pages that follow.

Cut 2 For Right Side
• Coupez 2 Pour le côté droit
Córtense 2 Para el lado derecho

Seam Line

Aysha and Ferny
July 3, 2006

For Aysha's grade 7 Home Ec.
class the kids were able to

pick a stuffed animal pattern to
sew up for their class project.

Aysha chose this cute
little elephant to make.

Lengthwise grain of fabric

McCALLS
656/8231
Men 15

erny

1 2 3 4 5 6 7 8 9 10 11 12

USING BITS AND PIECES from your sewing box gives you a wide array of items with which to embellish your pages. While looking for some buttons I came across a paper pattern for a clothing item that was well out-of-date. I knew I would never use it to make the garment, but I thought it would make the perfect patterned paper for adding a vintage look to chipboard letters. To use this lettering treatment as the central part of your design, simply trim the paper with a craft knife to fit over the large chipboard "F" and smaller chipboard letters. Add tape measure twill tape dyed with walnut ink, old buttons, safety pins and stickpins. My favorite finds from my sewing box for this page are the oversized hooks and eyes sewn in opposite corners in place of traditional photo anchors.

STRANGELY ENOUGH, OLD BUTTONS that I would never sew onto clothes are always my favorite for adding onto scrapbook pages and other paper crafts. After roughly trimming a heart from muslin, fill in the shape with various-sized buttons. My favorite button on this piece has a safety pin sewn to the middle and is raised with an adhesive foam square. After attaching the heart to a piece of hand-dyed muslin sewn to the base of the card, attach a decorative metal tag with a jump ring to the safety pin and secure it in place with another adhesive foam square. Add stickpins for a final touch to complete this vintage-style card.

AFTER COVERING CHIPBOARD LETTERS with an old paper pattern, I thought it would look cool to also use the pattern as part of the page foundation. Cover a piece of cream cardstock with the pattern (to strengthen it) and rather than combining it with cardstock or a patterned paper, dye a piece of Aida cloth in walnut ink for a perfect match. With a container of walnut ink handy, dip some sewing notions, labels and lace appliqués into the ink to make them match the heritage style of the page. Once dry, sew the zipper, Aida cloth and lace to the page. Complete the look with a collection of bobbin labels, needle packages, hook and eye cards and various finds from your sewing box.

Fabric

WHILE SCOURING THE AISLES of fabric at a local store, I came across this beautifully textured sheer fabric that I knew would match perfectly with this patterned paper and cute photo of my friend's daughter. Also, I thought the light weight of the fabric was perfectly suited for something young and playful. Begin by layering and sewing your papers to the page foundation. Once you've selected your fabric, trim it to make these unique chipboard page embellishments (see step-by-step instructions). After attaching the flowers to your page, trim strips of torn fabric to make stems to ground the flowers. Use zigzag stitching to match the stitching along the right side to pull the whole look together.

1 Trace a chipboard flower circle onto a piece of white cardstock, trim and set aside. Pop the flower out of the center of the chipboard flower circle. Apply adhesive to adhere a piece of patterned paper to the front of the chipboard circle; trim the patterned paper to fit. Ink the edge of the chipboard circle.

2 Adhere a piece of fabric to the underside of the chipboard circle. Do not pull the fabric too tight; you want to have enough fabric to pull up and make the flower "puffy." (I found that using a sticky dot adhesive works well as I can maneuver the fabric around until I am happy with the placement and how loose the fabric is in the center.)

3 Attach the white cardstock circle to the back of the fabric (use white cardstock so the true color of the sheer fabric will show). Decorate the small flower center with patterned paper and dimensional glaze. Adhere it to the middle of the fabric flower and "fluff" the fabric around it.

BEING A SCRAPBOOKER NATURALLY means I take lots of photographs. I love to surround my home with various photos of my family and friends, and a unique way to showcase these photos is to use my scrapbook supplies to create one-of-a-kind picture frames. This colorful frame is so easy to cover. Simply trim fabric strips into a variety of widths and weave them with coordinating ribbons for added contrast. The great thing about this finished frame is that because it opens up at the back (as opposed to the photo being permanently adhered to the front), you can easily change the photo whenever you please.

AS MUCH AS I love patterned paper, patterned fabric gives me even more creative options. As soon as I spotted this patterned upholstery fabric, I fell in love and knew I wanted to use it on a page. Begin by trimming your fabric to a 12" x 12" (30cm x 30cm) square. Then sew around the edge to frame your "page" and to prevent it from fraying. After sewing on the contrasting fabric and photograph, add layers of lace, velvet ribbon and twill. Cut one of the shapes from some of the scrap fabric and add pearly pink dimensional paint and a heart charm to evoke a soft feeling.

AS SOON AS I downloaded these photos into my computer I knew I had the perfect paper to scrapbook them with. The floral design of the paper reminded me of lace doilies and inspired me to dig into my extensive lace collection (which is a bit of an obsession of mine) to make my own lace flower embellishments. After layering and sewing your papers together, add your photos and journaling. Create the lace flower embellishments using lace and rhinestones (see step-by-step instructions) for the perfect addition. Adhere an additional strip of cotton lace along the right side to balance the design and pull the whole look together.

1 For a medium size flower, trim a 5" (13cm) piece of scalloped lace. With matching thread, sew a running stitch along the top edge of the lace.

2 Pull both ends of thread together to tightly gather the lace. Tie a knot to secure.

3 If needed, adhere the two ends of lace together to complete the flower. Add a decorative brad to the center of the flower to finish.

YOU MAY NOT AUTOMATICALLY think of lace when deciding on which products to use for scrapbooking photographs of a cat, but if you want to soften a pet page while conveying a feeling of love and affection, lace is the perfect texture to include. Notice how even though I combined three distinctly different styles of lace, my choice of colors, fonts and other page embellishments creates a cohesive look and prevents the page from becoming too "frilly." Select your own unique combination of lace to adorn a pet page, and the results are sure to please.

technique tips

As pretty as lace is all on its own, sometimes it can be fun to jazz it up a bit. Dye cotton lace in the same manner as fabric, or try one of the following ideas.

Weave narrow lengths of ribbon through the evenly spaced holes in the lace (fig. 1).

Use lace with a salvage edge to fold over to the front or sew down to create additional layers. Adhere eyelash fiber to show from underneath to add even more interest (fig. 2).

Add rhinestones, beads or glitter glue to the openings in the lace (fig. 3).

fig. 1

fig. 2

fig. 3

Grade 2   June 2004

Year end fun day at Cloverdale Elementary

annie
banannie

Cloverdale

Photo: Sandra Ash

I DON'T KNOW ANY scrapbooker who has not yet been bitten by the ribbon bug and has their own ever-growing stash of colorful ribbons. When my friend Sandra gave me this cute photo of her daughter Annie to scrapbook, I knew that bright, playful ribbons would be the perfect embellishment. Layer various lengths and widths of colorful ribbons in a vertical position against the stark contrast of white cardstock to add visual interest and bring out the colors in your photo. Add two funky flowers to the top right corner of the photo and the pink title in the lower right side of the page to make all the page elements perfectly balance.

NOT ALL RIBBONS ARE created equal. This is good news if you like to layer your ribbons on top of each other as I did on this cute page embellishment. Layer narrow rick-rack atop wider grosgrain ribbon and daisy trim on a wide-striped ribbon to spice up a blank chipboard base. Use glitter and pearly adhesives to add personality and charm. Simply apply a few drops of iridescent glitter glue to the center of the daisies for the perfect touch. If you don't have colored page pebbles at your disposal, adhere clear pebbles with small drops of liquid pearl adhesive in the color of your choice to turn them into your own custom mini page pebbles.

HAVE FUN WITH YOUR ribbons by creating dimensional shapes. To create the one in this example, trace a circle (or other shape) on the back of a piece of cardstock. Using a ⅜" (9mm) hole punch, punch evenly spaced holes throughout your shape. Trim a variety of 4" (10cm) coordinating ribbons, tie each ribbon with a loose knot in the center, and feed the ribbon tails through the hole from the front out to the back. Once you have all the holes filled with knots of ribbon, secure the ribbon tails to the back of the cardstock with adhesive.

Machine Sewing

THE EDGES OF PATTERNS on your papers are great places to add stitching for extra detail and visual interest. After selecting the patterned papers I wanted to use, I immediately wanted to sew inside the blue circles along the left side of the page. After attaching your patterned paper and photos, adhere the journaling and title letters with machine stitching. If you can't perfectly free-form stitch on your pages, select a computer font with hearts and print out the design on scrap paper. Then place it in the upper right corner of the page and sew each heart three times. Once finished, tear away the paper pattern to reveal the sewn image on your layout. Add stamped words, a sewn muslin paw print and a chipboard heart for a finishing touch.

STRIPED PAPER IS IDEAL for decorative stitching, and the printed lines also serve as a great guide if you are new to sewing. Sew across the front of your paper with a zigzag stitch. Sew lace to the underside of the right edge and then sew a straight stitch all around the edges of all the papers used for the cover. When sewing paper, keep your stitches longer than those you would sew on fabric because too many short stitches can perforate paper. Also, I recommend using dull needles from your stash for paper sewing because the paper will naturally dull them anyway. Save your sharp needles for fabric projects to avoid the expense of having to replace them.

Alex

June 2001

Alex (at 6 years old) playing in the school's playground during his Grade 1 year end fun day.

Prospect Lake

School

fun day

Ever since you started at PLS you have always loved playing on the dirt rocks with big ol' dump trucks and today was no exception!

MACHINE SEWING IS ONE of my favorite ways to add subtle texture to my pages. Plus, it's a great way to create visual balance through strategic arrangement and to help fill empty areas. If after trimming your papers and laying them down on your foundation it becomes apparent an area is not as visually "full" as you had anticipated, add extra interest by sewing a randomly spaced grid. Overlap the stitching onto the rest of the page to create a sense of unity.

THE **butterfly farm**

This being my second trip to Georgetown in Grand Cayman and the first time for the kids, I knew that the "must see" on the island was Stingray City to swim amongst the massive, but gentle stingrays. But when we arrived in Georgetown, the tour guides informed us that the water was quite rough out there today and that they only recommended it for strong swimmers. Although the kids can both swim, perhaps this might not be the best time to put them to the test, so we decided to take another excursion and settled on the Butterfly Farm. We have something similar to this here in Victoria, but still thought it would be a fun thing to do. So we all boarded the coach and drove out to the Butterfly Farm. After about a 15 minute drive we arrived at the farms

and met our tour guide. She told us that on September 12th 2004 Hurricane Ivan totally destroyed the farms and that after much rebuilding they opened up again that December. The Butterfly Farm was a beautiful, lush and tropical environment inside a large mesh "building" where hundreds of butterflies and moths freely fly around and feed on the plants and fruit. The Atlas Moths (top) were SO big and I love how their wings look like snakes. The little Banded Orange Butterflies (bottom right) were very pretty with their bright, vibrant colour and the Swallowtail Butterflies (bottom left) were such a delicate shape. So although this was not the same as swimming with stingrays, the Butterfly Farm was a great place to go and visit.

WHILE LOOKING THROUGH PHOTOGRAPHS of a recent trip to a butterfly farm, I suddenly got the great idea of adding pre-made fabric appliqué butterflies to a layout. Although I knew the appliqués would match the photos, I felt the layout still needed a certain flair. Hand-stitched flourishes that mimic delicate butterfly wings turned out to be the perfect handmade touch. Embroider the flourishes onto a cardstock background in the upper right and lower left corners (see step-by-step instructions) and add colorful brads. Adhere the appliqués and other decorative elements to your page. Trim narrow strips of cardstock to frame the page and to give it an extra dash of eye-popping color.

1 Stamp a flourish design along one edge of a piece of vellum or transparency. Stamp a second image to create a right-angle design that will fit in the corner of the page.

2 Using a temporary adhesive, attach the vellum so the pattern lines up in the corner of your page where you would like to place the stitched image. Place your page on a foam mat or mouse pad and use a needle to pierce evenly spaced stitching holes along the design.

3 Stitch the design using embroidery floss. Keep the pattern handy in case you need to refer to it as you stitch.

I ABSOLUTELY ADORE MY dog, Tia, so having made several mini books before but none about her, I thought one was long overdue. Because she is a girl I thought it would be fun to use a cute little flower-shaped book and girly colors.

To create the interior pages, take a piece of scrap paper and fold it in half. Place the spine of the book up against the fold, trace around the outline and then trim the pattern out. To make sure it fits the inside pages snugly, open up the pattern and slip it on top of the pages, making sure everything lines up properly. Then use the pattern to trim pages out of white and natural muslin.

After hand dying each of the fabric pages, sew around the edge with a running stitch and then embellish with photographs, ribbon, buttons, dog bone paper clips, a variety of flowers and rub-on words.

Paint each of the pages of the chipboard book with white acrylic paint. Once dry, adhere the completed cover and pages in place.

faMILY

love

Aysha, Alex and i

At Cheryl's dairy farm, Abbotsford, B.C.

Summer 2001

Moments like these are special, very special. We all get so busy with our lives, working too much, running errands and the like but why don't we make the time to just sit and be with each other? To spend precious time together while we can? Kids grow up so quickly and soon too will have full and busy lives and we will be the ones wanting them to sit with us and give us their time. Time to make special memories, to bond and be a family full of love, and i want to take advantage of each and every moment that i can.

USING HAND STITCHING ON layouts evokes a cozy, homespun feeling, which is what I wanted to convey on this sentimental page. Start with simple decorative stitching to secure hand-dyed fabric to pink cardstock. Use a basic running stitch to add color and detail to a felt flower and cardstock leaves. Add hand-stitched buttons and additional stitched flowers to create a visual triangle and pull the whole look together.

Silk Flowers

SILK FLOWERS ARE ONE of my favorite items to add to paper crafts, and I love the look that can be achieved with layering. To create this card's centerpiece, layer two silk flowers and punch a ⅜" (9mm) hole in the center. Next, take a 10" (25cm) length of wide ribbon, tie a loose knot in the center, and feed the ribbon tails down through the center of the flowers so the knot is positioned in the center. Attach the flowers to the center of a piece of cardstock, fold the ribbon tails to the back and secure. Put a few small drops of adhesive around the base of the ribbon knot and attach to the underside of the top flower so the flower is fuller. Finally, add purple crystals and iridescent glitter to the top flower for a little extra sparkle.

I LOVE DECORATING THE covers of mini albums because I don't have to be restricted by the size of my project. If I choose to, I can extend beyond every edge since my project doesn't need to fit inside a page protector. This worked out perfectly for layering these three gorgeous flowers across my fabric-covered album. Center a large pewter bookplate between the silk flowers with copper brads to secure the bookplate to the album cover. Use a chocolate-colored organza flower to delicately fill the center and apply drops of black glitter glue to add a soft richness.

I WAS WALKING THROUGH a superstore when I came across these huge silk flowers. As I looked at them I thought they would be perfect to pull apart and fill the background of a 12" x 12" (30cm x 30cm) page. Experiment by adding a pre-printed transparency atop a large flower. Layer ribbons and lace onto the background to fill some of the areas the flower does not. Stitch the flower to add extra detail and to also secure the petals firmly in place. Finally, trim your focal photo into a circle and add letters around the curved edge to continue the flow of the flower's shape.

technique tips

Plain silk flowers are a blank canvas just waiting to be decorated. The next time you're thinking of adding some to a page consider one of the following ideas:

- *Colorful mini brads*
- *Glitter and liquid pearl adhesives*
- *Rub-on images*
- *Stamped designs*

Fibers

MOST OF US HAVE used fibers to tie through the end of tags, wrap around letters and other similar techniques. But you can also create cool borders and strips, especially with variegated fibers. After making your fiber borders (see step-by-step instructions), add them to your page with a large photo, title and a second smaller photo. For some extra color, add a ribbon into the wider border strip and accent with a ribbon slide and antique copper brads. Pull elements from your photo into your type treatments. Notice how the textures of the wooden beams in my photo are played up by the similar pattern of the title letter stickers.

1 Trim a piece of chipboard to the size of your border and cover one side fully with double-sided tape.

2 Trim a long strip of fiber and place over the double-sided tape in a zigzag pattern until it is completely covered. Place each row of fiber as close as possible to each other to avoid gaps.

3 Once the chipboard is completely covered with fiber, trim the ends so the edges are straight and without loose strands. Attach to your page.

HeiDi

FRIENDS

Heidi and I instantly clicked from the first time photo we met each other at Camp Memory Makers in 2005 and she is one of my closest scrapbooking friends. Unfortunately though we couldn't live much further apart even if we tried, so whenever we're both attending the same trade show we always try to spend as much of our free time together as we can. MMM Dinner at CHA - W in Las Vegas

January 2006

tRUDY

THERE ARE SO MANY different types of beautiful fibers available on the market, and eyelash fibers are one of my personal favorites. By paying attention to detail and adding small amounts in strategically placed areas, you can add a beautifully soft texture to your page. A fun idea is to wrap a short length of eyelash fiber around the post of a brad before inserting it in the center of a silk flower. It's quick and easy, and it adds an elegance and richness that contributes to the overall look and feel of the page.

With all the times that I have been to Las Vegas I had never gone to Siegfried & Roy's Secret Garden at the Mirage. On this trip with Lonnie, we decided to go and walk through it. It was amazing and we loved Gildah, their Asian Elephant.

01/03

{Elephants}
Of The
Desert

metals 2

Wire

Wire Mesh

Hardware

Embossing Metal

Metal Moldings

Metal Letters and Words

Charms

Brads and Eyelets

ASK ANYONE WHO KNOWS me and they will tell you I love to scour the aisles of my local hardware store for all sorts of great metal finds to use on scrapbook pages. When you first think of metal you probably envision something industrial, hard, cold and dramatic, and although it can certainly be all of these things, it is a remarkably versatile material. It can be cut, embossed, crimped, pierced, inked and painted. Using any of these techniques can dramatically change the mood and texture of metal while the process of altering can take your creativity to a whole new level. It's likely you've already incorporated metals into your projects with brads, eyelets and charms. So why not take a look around your house or in your toolbox to see what other metal treasures you might find?

As you flip though the pages of this chapter you will notice the diverse mood and feeling in the layouts and projects. They include fun and playful, clean and graphic, rough and rugged, heritage and shabby—all with metal as the common thread that binds them together. Learn how to incorporate a variety of metal items on your scrapbook pages to give your them that extra punch of visual creativity.

YOU CAN FIND UNIQUE items to use on scrapbook pages in the most unexpected places. As I was shopping in a home décor store, I came across a package of wire animal-shaped paper clips in the clearance section that I knew would be perfect for a selection of elephant photos I had at home. If you're looking to use wire in a new way, try this variation of a traditional machine-stitched border. Feed lengths of 24-gauge black wire through a paper crimper and adhere to your page using liquid adhesive. It's quick and easy and provides the perfect finishing touch to an exotic page.

technique tips

Working with wire can be tricky when trying to figure out what gauge—or thickness—you should use. The larger the number, the thinner and more pliable the wire is. The smaller the number, the thicker and more firm the wire is. I prefer to use 24-gauge for scrapbooking because it is flexible enough to bend and shape, but firm enough to hold that shape once created.

WHEN CREATING RUGGED AND outdoor style pages, select a type of wire that reflects that mood. I decided that 22-gauge wire with a faux rust finish was the perfect choice to make rusty barbed wire borders for this page. Wrap a length of wire around one of the chipboard letters to convey the feeling of wire on a fence post. This not only helps support the feeling of nature, but also pulls the design and barbed wire borders together.

1 Trim three 12" (30cm) lengths of rust-colored wire and twelve 3" (8cm) lengths of regular wire.

2 Twist together the three 12" (30cm) lengths so they form one piece.

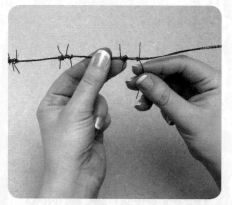

3 Leaving a ³/₈" (9mm) tail, wrap one of the 3" (8cm) lengths of wire around the larger piece. Wrap it three times and trim the tail to ³/₈" (9mm). Add a second piece of wire next to the first. Leave 2" (5cm) in space and repeat. (If your wrapped wire begins to slip, tap it on the back with a hammer.)

Wire Mesh

1 Apply a rub-on flower to a piece of transparency. Fill in the petals with colored dimensional glaze and let dry.

2 Use a 1/8" (3mm) hole punch to create a hole in the center.

3 Use a brad to attach the flower to a piece of metal mesh.

WIRE MESH IS A fun and unexpected way to add texture to your pages. It's inexpensive, adds little to no bulk, and only requires wire cutters or an old pair of scissors to trim it (just remember to protect your eyes from small bits that may fly up while cutting!). If you're going for a playful and funky look, combine wire screening and doodle-style rub-on flowers for a unique embellishment. Add stapled photo corners for subtle touches of metal throughout your page.

technique tips

You can easily alter the look of your mesh with a quick coat of paint, solvent-based ink (I recommend Staz-on by Tsukineko), or embossing powder. Then leave as is or give a quick rub with some sandpaper to further enhance the look.

4 Carefully trim around the flower through both the transparency and metal mesh. Undo the metal prong in the brad and use it to secure the flower to your page.

JUST LIKE WIRE, METAL mesh comes in a range of thicknesses. For this page, I decided larger, more industrial mesh was perfect for this rugged page. After you create the page background, attach strips of mesh with washers and screw brads to create a textural border and strip. Tip: Stamping on embossed cardstock is a great way to emphasize textures found in your photographs as illustrated here with the title word "Jungle" and the vehicle's tires.

Hardware

It's funny how a good friend can be right there in front of your face but you just don't see them yet, that is how it was with Sandra and I. We both knew who the other was but had never really talked to each other until I had to go to Scrapbook Source's warehouse in Calgary to design my classes for the CCHA trade show. Since Sandra was on their design team, they were also bringing her out to help prep my classes. We were both nervous about traveling and having to spend so much time with someone we didn't know, but we had not even been at the airport for five minutes when we felt like long lost friends. And now, 2 and a half years later, we can't imagine our lives with out the other one in it. (Photo - June 3 '06)

Photo: Cate Shepherd

THESE 3" (8cm) METAL corner brackets were so much fun to use on this shabby and feminine page. Experiment with painting or sanding them to add a distressed look. The pre-made holes work perfectly for securing the bracket to your page with screw brads, or tying with twine or ribbon. Spiky washers work great as the perfect centers for flowers and contrast well with the other metal embellishments. These washers come in all sizes so you are sure to find the right one to fit and add sparkle to any silk or paper flowers you have in your stash.

METAL TINS CAN BE fun to customize so I made this one as a special place to keep handwritten notes from my son. First, decorate the lid with patterned paper, paint and fabric. Use an awl to pierce through the lid to make two holes for screw top brads that will attach a hinge. Decorate both sides of a chipboard square with additional papers, wire mesh and chipboard letters. Adhere a bracket to the edge of the square's right side and then attach the square to the hinge on the left with screw top brads to permanently attach it to the tin. Tie a strip of muslin and a metal charm through the bracket as a handle to flip up the square to reveal a hidden photograph and journaling.

Alex,
You are the sweetest boy that any mother could hope for and I am so lucky to have you. This tin is a special place for me to keep some of the sweet notes that you have written to me so that I can treasure them always.
Love,

technique tips

Metal brackets work well on a wide variety of page styles. Try one of these creative options.

Paint and sand a bracket (see layout on page 34).

Cover a metal bracket with distress embossing powders and finish with screw top brads (fig. 1).

Paint a bracket and, once dry, apply rub-ons. Finish off with antique brads (fig. 2).

Apply alcohol ink to a bracket and finish with ornate nail heads (fig. 3). (I adhered the nail heads onto the tops of brads and easily secured them through the holes of the brackets.)

Cover a bracket with patterned paper, sand the edges and set eyelets through the holes (fig. 4).

fig. 1

fig. 2

fig. 3

fig. 4

shamu

SEAWorld

Living on the southern coast of British Columbia we are often lucky enough to see pods of Killer Whales swimming in the Strait of Georgia while we ride the ferry over to Vancouver. However, no trip to Sea World would be complete with out seeing Shamu and the other Killer Whales that live at the park. They have an amazing set up and their large tank is so cool with observation windows underground so that you can see them swim underwater. Another thing that I thought was pretty cool was seeing the interaction between the trainers and the whales during their show. You could see that there was so much trust there (on both sides) as they swam together and as the whales threw their trainers up in the air with their snouts, it looked as if they were having as much fun as each other.   November 2004, Orlando, Florida.

MANY CRAFTERS FEEL INTIMIDATED by the idea of using embossing metal sheets, but they are actually remarkably easy to use. This page was about the whales at Seaworld in Orlando, so I thought embossing metal with a variety of circles (see step-by-step instructions) would complement the page perfectly. Alcohol inks and mini page pebbles finished off the watery background, and large chipboard letters covered with a layer of dimensional glaze complete the page.

 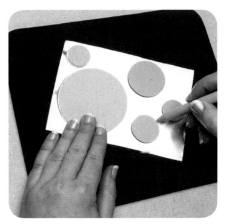 

1 Adhere chipboard circles to the back of an embossing metal sheet.

2 Place the metal sheet, chipboard side up, on a mouse pad or nail head mat. Use an embossing stylus or paper stump to trace around the edge of each circle.

3 Flip the metal sheet over so the chipboard side is down. Again, trace around the edge of the chipboard to further define the circles. Finish off with alcohol inks and pearl mixatives (see page 76 for step-by-step instructions).

I would thank you from the bottom of my heart, but for you my heart has no bottom.

Unknown

SCRAP PIECES FROM METAL sheets can be ideal for smaller page embellishments and cards. This metal tile only takes a few minutes to make with the use of a handy die-cut system. After you trim and emboss the tile, apply a layer of chalk ink. Work the ink into the recessed areas and then wipe the surface clean with a paper towel. Finally, apply a coat of dimensional glaze to seal the ink and provide a high-shine finish.

METAL MOLDINGS ARE A unique way to add texture and interest to your scrapbooking and paper craft projects. They are available in many different widths and patterns. You can use them as is, or apply paint, ink, metallic rub-ons, embossing powders or alcohol inks to color them and bring out their embossed designs. Because they are generally made from a thinner grade of metal, they are easy to cut and use as smaller strips as I did on this box book. Simply apply a coat of paint, wait for it to partially dry and then wipe with a paper towel. That's all it takes to alter a metal molding that will perfectly complement the cover of a mini album or other project.

Idwal & Edith Evans
November 13th, 1963

When I think of my grandparents, I picture them like this as they are here in this photo. I'm not quite sure why as I was not even born when it was taken, but maybe as my grandfather passed away 6 years later, this is the photo I have seen the most of the two of them together. This day would have been a very special one for them as they were celebrating their Ruby wedding anniversary. 40 years, quite an accomplishment and something I can't even imagine... especially since I'm not even 40 years old myself yet. But as I look through old photos of my grandparents and I see them posed all prim and proper, one thing is evident, they loved each other very much and were lucky enough to spend 40 happy years together.

True

LOVE

MOLDING STRIPS CAN ALSO be an ideal embellishment for heritage pages such as this one. If you choose patterned papers that have a distressed look, your metal moldings should have the same feel. To achieve this look, coat the metal strips with a layer of metallic black paint. Once dry, complete the aging process by distressing with a piece of sandpaper. Add a similarly treated hand-embossed square tile to pull the whole design together.

Imagine fun family

Dream cherish

process

Hope

Believe togetherness

{ "We never know the love of our parents for us until we have
become parents ourselves." - Henry Ward Beecher
Mum, Dad and I, Christmas 2002 }

METAL WORDS CAN
CREATE interesting borders
or mats especially when they
are combined with other art
mediums such as texture
paste (see step-by-step
instructions). Add simple
journaling and stitched border strips to keep your page
clean and clutter-free and to
keep the emphasis on the
photo and sentimental words.

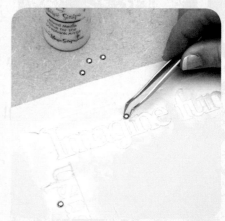

1 Center the photograph on the page and
lightly trace around it with a pencil.
Arrange and adhere the metal words so they
frame the photo mat.

2 Apply texture paste over the metal words
and scrape the letters clear, making sure to
leave clumps of paste around the edges. Let the
paste dry. (I hung mine with clothes pins to
dry so the page would not ripple as much from
the moisture in the texture paste.)

3 Once the page is dry, use wire cutters to
trim the backs off five silver brads. Tap the
backs with a hammer to flatten the remaining
bits of metal prongs (this will allow your brad
top to adhere more securely). Adhere one brad
top to the dot above each letter "i" in the
words spaced around the edge of the photo.

If there is one thing that is evident it's that Alex loves the beach, so he is always excited for when Dean has his annual "Sawyer's Family BBQ". The BBQ is always at Dean's house, which is right on the beach so it means an afternoon playing in the sand, riding his boat out to check the crab traps (with a detour around the bay) and jumping on the trampoline, plus there are always tons of other kids there for him to play with. This time they also had big bubble wands for the kids to play with so after dinner, once the younger kids were getting tired and the bubble wands were free, Alex managed to sneak down on the beach and have a go with them. As a breeze was blowing in just the right direction, he was trying to aim them just right so that they would pop on his grandpa's head as he was sat on a chair chatting to the other guests. Ah, to be a kid again!

7/09/06

ON THE BEACH

ALEX

MY SON HAD SO much fun playing with a big bubble wand on the beach this day that I wanted my page to reflect that same carefree feeling. Intertwine wavy strips of patterned papers with each other and with shimmery vellum circles adorned with small metal letters. Add clear round buttons to subtly support a bubble or water theme. Add metal letters distressed with paint and dimensional glaze to finish off the weathered look of a beach or outdoor page.

March 2004

Georgetown,
The Grand Cayman Is.
Taking a boat ride out to Sting Ray C...

Out of all of the islands in the Caribbean the Grand Cayman Is. were by far my favorite as it was so pretty there. I went back a year later after Hurricane Ivan had been through and although they had done well to rebuild, it was still so sad to see just how much had been damaged.

NOT ALL CHARMS NEED to dangle from jump rings or pretty bows. Don't be afraid to cut their loops off with wire cutters and tuck them into little places around your page to help support its theme. Small fish, starfish and sand dollar charms are ideal embellishments to be caught up amongst all of the netting and cheesecloth in a highly textural coastal page like this one.

Tia is just the cutest dog ever! When ever the kids and I go to Beaver or Elk Lake

for a walk she always likes to come along and be part of everything. The second

we sit down for a break, she's in there straight away with kisses full of gratitude.

tia,

MY

SWEET GIRL

July 20th, 2003

CHARMS HAVE LONG BEEN one of my favorite embellishments to add on my scrapbook pages. Use them to add subtle reinforcement of your page's theme (as I did with the charms that dangle from my page). You can also use them to create visual triangles and achieve a sense of balance in your design. This page would look a little empty if it were lacking the three charms that perfectly adorn it.

technique tips

I must admit that I am a bit of a charm addict, but even so, I don't always have the right charm in just the right color of metal. This can easily be corrected with metallic leafing pens. The original color of the star charms shown here is pewter, but coloring them with either a silver, gold or copper leafing pen and wiping away the excess ink results in the perfect shade of metal for my charm.

I FEEL THAT BRADS are one of the most overlooked items in a scrapbooker's toolkit. Instead of employing them only for their functional purpose of securing items together, get creative and use them for decorative purposes or to add the perfect finishing touch to any style of page. After painting chipboard flourishes with metallic pearl paint, simple silver brads add a clean line elegance and complete the look of this exotic page.

THE ADDITION OF ITEMS such as eyelets framing holes on your embellishments or scrapbook page is something so simple but really adds the finishing touch that makes your layouts look more polished. You can also cut the backs off brads so that you can place them at the ends of ribbon without causing snags, or metal molding strips that you can't pierce through, as illustrated here.

May 2004

Ahh Chloe, what a cutie you are! You come running into the scrapbook store with your Mum Cate, all happy and excited to see everyone like it's your second

home. Often you are sporting one of your new outfits that Cate has just bought you (and although we think she's crazy, we have to admit that you do look pretty darn cute!) Cate brings your bed and your ball for you and you wonder why the customers

don't want to play while your Mum is busy working. I guess they just don't know that you are the unofficial mascot of Memory Lane Scrapbooking!

Princess Chloe

PLAYFUL PATTERNED PAPERS AND colorful brads and eyelets are perfect for a fun pet page. Use eyelets to make up the foundation of a unique flower embellishment (see step-by-step instructions) and add a grouping of brads to accent. Add an abundance of stitching, sequin hearts, staples and ribbons to provide additional pretty details for an untraditional pet page.

Photo: Cate Shepherd

1 Place a button on the page and make six evenly spaced marks around the button for the ⅜"(9mm) eyelets. Make six more evenly spaced marks around the button for the ⅛"(3mm) eyelets. Punch out the holes with the correct size of anywhere hole punches.

2 Set all of the eyelets. Cut six 4" (10cm) lengths of ribbon. Fold one piece in half and poke the folded end though the ⅜" (9mm) eyelet hole and adhere the ribbon ends to the back. Repeat with the five remaining lengths of ribbon and ⅜" (9mm) eyelets.

3 Use double-sided tape to adhere a circle of Angelina Fiber to the center of the flower. Decorate the button with an inked chipboard circle and brads. Attach it on top of the fiber using foam adhesive.

saturna

Alex and I on Saturna Island.
Grade 4 bike trip. June 2004.

Having lived on the coast of
somewhere most of my life. I love

the way old storm weathered
buildings look. They have so much

charm and personality. just like
this house on Saturna Island.

island

natural elements 3

Flowers and Leaves

Mica

Burlap

Cork

Wood

Sandpaper

Hemp Twine and Twill

Marauyma Mesh

NOTHING IS QUITE SO incredible as what can be found in nature. Our surroundings truly are a sight to behold: beautiful beaches with crystal clear waters, jagged mountains covered in snow, brilliant colors of delicately shaped flowers and fields of tall grass dancing in the wind. How vastly different the sights, smells and textures of each of them are and how lucky we are to have them as they make our world a more interesting place. So as you start to notice and think about the textures in the world around us, you will start to become more aware of the textures you are capturing in your photographs. What better way to enhance them than to pull some of those same textures onto your scrapbook pages.

Throughout the pages of this chapter we will get back to basics and explore all that nature has to offer and how we can incorporate these highly tactile items into our scrapbooks. Keep in mind that because these are natural items many of them contain acid and lignin and therefore are not archival.

Flowers and Leaves

A little birdie told me
today's your special day
I hope that it is perfect
in each and every way.
Have a joyous celebration
with loved ones ever near
and tender hugs and kisses
to last though out the year.
My wish for you is happiness
and all your dreams come true
for there is no other person
who deserves it more than you.

- Rose Marie Streeter

THIS DELICATE FLOWER IS not only well protected but a beautiful embellishment for any paper craft project. Adhere a flower to a microscope slide and place a second microscope slide on top. Seal the two slides together by wrapping a thin strip of double-sided tape around the edges of the slides. Peel off the tape's protective backing, apply metallic leafing flakes to the adhesive and brush off any excess. To finish off the embellishment, add a strip of white cardstock to the back of the slide.

MANY DRIED FLOWERS AND leaves, by their very nature, have a wonderfully elegant look to them. Layer them on handmade paper and mica tiles with liquid adhesive and then wrap them with twine to help emphasize their natural beauty. You can attach the finished flower tiles to adorn a classic greeting card as I did here, or to vintage papers as a unique scrapbook page embellishment.

Sisters

Kara and Jenna
August 21, 2005

A younger sister is someone to use as a guinea-pig in trying sledges and experimental go-carts. Someone to send on messages to Mum.

But someone who needs you - who comes to you with bumped heads, grazed knees, tales of persecution.

Someone who trusts you to defend her. Someone who thinks you know the answers to almost everything.
- Pam Brown

DRIED FLOWERS ARE ONE of my favorite embellishments to use when creating delicate, feminine or heritage style scrapbook pages. Because dried flowers are extremely fragile, use a few drops of liquid adhesive to securely attach them to smaller items, such as vellum tags, so you can move them around until you find the perfect position for them on your layout. Attaching them to tags popped up with adhesive foam creates an additional buffer to slow down any damage from acid migration.

MICA TILES ARE THIN, flexible pieces of the mineral mica that naturally forms in layers. They work great for scrapbooking because you can separate the layers and have variation with the intensity of colors. Mica is also able to withstand high temperatures, making it an ideal surface for heat embossing. In this example, the mica tiles worked perfectly for replicating the stone inukshuk in the photo and also provided me with the perfect placement for my title, which was stamped with a solvent-based ink due to the title's slick and non-porous surface.

technique tips

Like vellum, the clear properties of mica can make it tricky to attach without adhesive showing. Clear-drying liquid adhesive works well but you need to use a small amount and ensure that it dries without air bubbles (those will be visible once dry). Also, because mica is non-porous it will take longer for the adhesive to dry clear.

MICA IS AN IDEAL material for layering images and text because the tiles are transparent and can be separated into multiple layers. Create different type treatments by stamping an image or printing it on cardstock or transparency and then covering it up with a layer of mica to create a natural smoky look (see step-by-step instructions). Mica can also work to reinforce your page's theme. On this layout about my irrational fear of fire, I wanted the tiles to look like rocks or wood in front of a burning fire.

Photos: Shannon Taylor

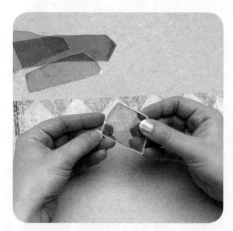

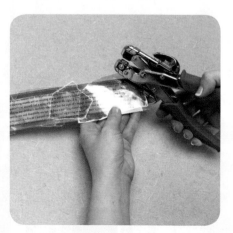

1 Trim a 2½" x 11¾" (6cm x 30cm) strip of patterned paper. Add a border sticker to the top and bottom edges of the paper strip. Select the mica tiles you want to use and separate each of the tiles into two pieces by pushing your fingernail into the corner of the tile until it separates and you can pull it apart.

2 Adhere one set of tiles to the patterned paper strip. For a more natural look, allow the mica to hang over the edges of the strip. Print journaling onto a transparency and attach to the mica border. (This technique also looks great using a photograph printed on photo paper or on a transparency.)

3 Adhere the remaining tiles (be sure to match up the pairs) on top of the transparency. Use a hole punch to make two ⅛" (3mm) holes at both ends and attach a large brad through each of the holes.

November 2004

OK, I would never normally call my Mum crazy, but in this case it's true. After our cruise finished and we disembarked in Miami, we decided to stay an extra day and take the kids to the Everglades. After watching one of the shows at Gatorland, people were allowed to hold one of the alligators and Mum really wanted to do it. So I know it's a "smaller" sized gator and

that it's mouth is taped shut, but you still won't catch me doing it. So yep, I think my Mum is crazy!

GATORLAND

BURLAP IS AVAILABLE IN several different shades and weaves and can be purchased in small, pre-cut rolls, like the 6" (15cm) strips I used here, or by the yard just like other fabrics. After combining several distressed papers to create the foundation of your page, layer them with strips of loose weave burlap. Adhere the burlap with double-sided tape that can be easily hidden under your photographs and by a muslin strip like the one I have sewn on top. Add small drops of liquid adhesive to secure any loose areas or fraying ends.

THIS LIGHT-COLORED, TIGHTLY WOVEN burlap provided me with the texture I wanted for this page, but when placed with my other items I found it was too flat and stark in color. To tone it down and bring more of a decorative element to the page, place an adhesive mask on the burlap and paint over it with a coat of chocolate-colored paint. Once dry, it will be the perfect addition to any layout, and the painted design will help to fill in empty areas of the page.

technique tips

Burlap doesn't always need to be hidden or layered under strips of patterned papers or photographs. Let it take center stage and give it a bit more personality by trying one of these ideas.

Place a mask over the burlap and apply an ageing varnish (or use paint as I did on the "Saturna Island" layout above). Once dry, ink and sew the edges and apply a rub-on phrase (fig. 1).

Transfer a rub-on to the burlap and apply dimensional glaze to part of the image as I did to the small heart in the center. Decorate with a chipboard frame and add another layer of glaze (fig. 2).

Stamp a border design with a solvent-based ink. Decorate the center with a chipboard heart and grosgrain ribbon (fig. 3).

Ink the edges with distress ink and stitch a border. Add dried flowers for a rustic touch (fig. 4).

fig. 1

fig. 2

fig. 3

fig. 4

CORK IS AN IDEAL textural material for an abundance of pages. It works perfectly for fall, nature, camping and beach themes just to name a few. Cork is available in paper thin sheets making it extremely easy to work with. You can trim it into the size and shape of your choosing with a scissors, craft knife or rotary trimmer. Although you can shade cork the traditional way using ink, try experimenting with a wood-burning tool to create a more authentic feel (see step-by-step instructions).

1 Adhere the chipboard letters, opposite side up, to the back of a sheet of cork.

2 Use a craft knife to carefully trim each letter.

3 Pre-heat the burning tool according to the manufacturer's instructions. Once heated, carefully hold the chipboard letter with tweezers and rub the burning tool back and forth along the edges until you achieve the desired amount of shading.

As we were walking around Old Field Farms for their Octoberfest celebration, we came across a hay maze which you had to go in. As you were crawling through you found a window in the maze that you popped your head out of so you could say hi to me.

at the PATCH

10/01

WITH SO MUCH VISUAL texture in this photograph, I knew it was safe for me to have fun playing around with this design while still achieving a well-balanced look. Trim a sheet of cork into 1" (3cm) strips, use a wood-burning tool to shade the edges and sew them to the page. Vary it up a bit by sewing one set of strips with frayed muslin peeking out from underneath. Use fiber, twill, ribbon and vintage looking tags to achieve a rustic look. Notice how although the page is heavily embellished, the photo still takes center stage. Trim the cork strips so they become smaller as they reach the center, framing your photo with different textiles and placing the tags so they all point to the center.

INSPIRED BY THE COMBINATION of light-colored wood and brushed metal found on kitchen cupboards, this sheet of maple paired with metal mesh was the perfect material for my contemporary page design. Because the wood is paper-thin it can easily crack along the grain of the wood, but you can still carefully punch holes and set eyelets into it as I did here. Add lightly inked textured cardstock, natural twill tape and touches of twine for perfect finishing touches to a coastal-themed page like this one.

TAKE A WALK DOWN the aisles of any craft store and you will surely come across a section filled with wooden shapes perfect for adding to your scrapbook and paper craft projects. To create an embellishment similar to the large flower on this mini book, stain a wooden flower with a layer of walnut ink and then embellish with fabric strips, a large brad and mini paper flowers. Trim a paper-thin sheet of wood with a die-cutting system to create unique photo anchors. Put them together with distressed papers, cheesecloth and an abundance of ribbons to create a wonderfully rustic design.

WOOD MESH, LIKE THE type used on this wildlife page, creates wonderful textures for natural-themed pages. To achieve a looser, more open weave, dampen the strip and then pull apart the grains of the wood. Once you are happy with the results, let the wood dry. (To speed this process up, lay it on a sheet of tin foil and place it out in the sun to dry.) Because the wood mesh has so much texture, it may look out of place when layered on top of regular cardstock. Use handmade paper for the foundation and layer it with a distressed sheet of cork to provide enough texture to create a balance with the visual weight of the wood.

8/11/02

One of Aysha's favorite parts of going to a BBQ at Dean's house is being able to go out on his boat.

While out in the bay he'll stop at his several crab traps to see what he's managed to catch so

far. The kids like to try and guess how many crabs are in the traps and how many of those are

large enough to keep. Dean also always shows the kids how to tell by the crabs markings if they are

male or female. As for the adults back on shore, they just like being able to eat the day's catch!

Catching

SANDPAPER HAS A WONDERFUL texture that can be used in many ways to enhance your pages—and I don't just mean by killing your arm sanding! Begin by creating your page foundation with weathered wood patterned paper and a piece of fish netting. Next, combine sandpaper with distressed sponge stamps to create the perfect weathered title (see step-by-step instructions). Cover the letters with dimensional glaze to give your letters extra shine and to also smooth out the roughness of the sandpaper so it won't scratch a page protector in your album.

1 Slightly dampen a sponge stamp with water and then cover with a light coat of paint (dampening the stamp helps produce a better image). Press the stamp onto the sandpaper to create your image.

2 Using on old pair of scissors, cut out all of the letters. Ink around the edge of each letter with a black inkpad.

3 Securely attach the letters to your page and then cover each letter with an even layer of dimensional glaze. Let dry for several hours.

ALTHOUGH I LOVE TO tie little bits of twine and place them in random patterns all around my layouts, it has more creative uses. The flower stems in the patterned paper inspired me to use twine for decorative stems and vines on this page. Use this material to give your layout directional lines to help guide the viewer's eye around the page. This technique also works as a great replacement for traditional machine-stitched borders and directional lines.

TWILL TAPE AND HEMP twine worked perfectly to embellish this rustic Alaskan page. After layering subtle patterned papers with burlap and adding decorative stitching, sew a narrow strip of patterned paper to a 1" (3cm) strip of twill to create a border for your title to "rest" on. Instead of using typical page additions (the good ol' photo anchor), visually secure your photos to the page by setting an eyelet in the corner of the photo or journaling block and then wrap smooth twine threaded with metallic beads.

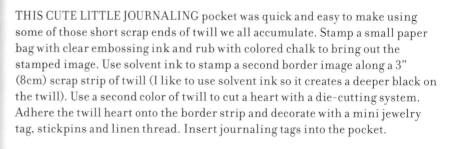

THIS CUTE LITTLE JOURNALING pocket was quick and easy to make using some of those short scrap ends of twill we all accumulate. Stamp a small paper bag with clear embossing ink and rub with colored chalk to bring out the stamped image. Use solvent ink to stamp a second border image along a 3" (8cm) scrap strip of twill (I like to use solvent ink so it creates a deeper black on the twill). Use a second color of twill to cut a heart with a die-cutting system. Adhere the twill heart onto the border strip and decorate with a mini jewelry tag, stickpins and linen thread. Insert journaling tags into the pocket.

MESH, WHETHER IN STRIPS or in sheets like the Maruyama mesh used on this page, is an ideal product to add an abundance of texture to your page but with no more bulk than a sheet of cardstock. It's great for bringing more visual interest to areas that you want to leave as a relatively open space and for filling in areas where you want a more layered look. This page about my pampered cat illustrates the use of both of these techniques.

June 3rd, 2006

Cate

Sandra

Trudy

Julia

Tsawwassen Ferry Terminal

Who needs an excuse to go on a scrapbooking road trip? Not us, so when I asked Cate, Sandra and Julia if they wanted to come on a road trip so I could look for stuff to use in my new book, they didn't need to be asked twice! We got up early and took the ferry over to Vancouver and then headed across the border and to our favorite store in Bellingham and then back up to several stores in the Lower Mainland. Cate was so funny, because I couldn't tell anyone yet what the the topic of my book was about

road trip

she had to look every time I bought something to see if she could guess what it was about from what I was buying (not knowing that the things that would give it away was coming directly from the manufacturers!) So after a full day of shopping we rode the ferry back to Victoria and passed the time with a "show & tell" of everything each of us had bought. Before too long the one and a half hour ferry ride was over and we were all back at home.

ALTHOUGH MESH IS AVAILABLE in an abundance of colors, you can easily customize it with inks and dyes to achieve the perfect shade. I recommend choosing a subtle white mesh to layer with bold patterned papers. Trim a flower from the mesh so you can layer it and create more texture for a large paper flower. Lightly ink the edges of the mesh flower with chalk ink and place it on top of the chipboard button secured with pretty ribbon.

art mediums 4

Crackle

Texture Paste

Air-Dry Clay

Transfer Ink

Paper Perfect

Alcohol Inks

Metallic Flakes

Batik Resist Medium

Adirondack Wash

THE WORD TEXTURE CAN be broken down and defined as two different types—visual texture and tactile texture. Tactile texture is used to define three dimensional items; it is how something actually feels. Is its surface rough, smooth, soft or lumpy? You can tell this sort of texture by actually touching the item or by how it catches the light and casts shadows. Visual texture defines two dimensional items and if you were to touch the surface, it would be flat and smooth even though it looks like it should be otherwise. A good example of this is a photograph of a rocky beach. Its visual texture makes it look rough and jagged, but if you were to touch the photograph it is actually smooth. The old master artists have long known and experimented with the differences between visual and tactile texture and would add tactile texture to their paintings by building up the layers of paint or by adding sand into their mixture.

Fortunately for today's artists there are many different art mediums on the market that easily aid us in creating different kinds of texture that can be incorporated into our scrapbooks. In this chapter I invite you to revisit those long gone days of high school art class as we learn how to create both visual and tactile texture with a variety of art mediums.

Crackle

AS I WALKED THROUGH the aisles of this outdoor market I was surrounded by contrasting textures: torn fabric canopies, rough wooden support beams and ripped crumpled boxes next to the smooth shiny skins of the peppers, tomatoes and other fruits and vegetables. What better backdrop for these photographs than to replicate some of these very textures on my layout. Crackle medium is great for creating beautiful rough textures but can often buckle lighter weight papers. Paint crackle medium onto an overhead transparency to prevent any buckling and to give you a completely flat surface to work with. Add epoxy bubble letters and dimensional glaze on a chipboard title to provide contrast with items in your photographs.

1 Paint a piece of transparency with an even layer of crackle finish. Let the crackle dry until it is tacky to the touch. If it dries too much, the next layer of paint will not crack properly. Also note that the direction of your brush strokes determine the direction of your crackling.

Tip: Place a small sticky note in the corner of the transparency so you have something to hold on to as you paint.

2 Paint over the tacky crackle finish with an acrylic paint (I find that a matte finish paint works better than glossy paint). The cracks will start to appear and will take a few minutes to completely finish.

3 Once the paint is thoroughly dry, brush over the paint with a layer of antiquing gel to stain the paint and create more depth to your finished piece. Use a soft, dry cloth to wipe away any excess gel.

CRACKLE MEDIUM CAN BE used for more than just rustic looking pages; you can also use it for delicate, feminine pages similar to the one shown here. If you're going to cover the majority of your cardstock with crackle and paint, there's a possibility it will buckle the cardstock. To prevent this, attach the cardstock to a sheet of chipboard so it will have more body. After the foundation crackles, add additional "delicate" items to complete the softness of your page.

Alaska

Watching a glacier carve is an amazing experience. First you hear the thunderous sound of ice cracking followed by the magnificent sight of massive chunks of ice falling into the ocean. We were fortunate to see lots of carving during our visit to Hubbard Glacier.

Hubbard Glacier

carving

Photo: Phyllis Wright

I LOVE THE COOL jaggedness of the ice in this photo and knew that with texture paste I could create ideal page embellishments to perfectly complement the image. Also, I didn't want to distract from the beautiful colors of the glacier by adding a patterned paper with multiple colors. I decided black would be the best choice to allow the true colors to really shine forth. To prevent the white texture paste tiles from becoming too overpowering, I mixed in blue mica flakes to tone down the white.

1 Squeeze a small amount of texture paste (similar in size to a grape) onto the chipboard tile.

2 Sprinkle mica flakes onto the paste and mix together with a palette knife. Spread the mixture evenly on the tile and dab with the palette knife to make mini "mountain peaks."

3 Sprinkle on a few more mica flakes for extra sparkle. Let dry for several hours before adding it to your page.

CHIPBOARD TILES ARE PERFECT foundations for creating page and mini book embellishments. Trace around a 5" (13cm) chipboard tile on a piece of transparency and trim. Spread a layer of texture paste onto one corner of the transparency square and stamp into the paste with a foam stamp. While the texture paste is drying, create the remainder of the tile with layered patterned papers, stickers and a photograph. Because the texture paste design is on transparency, you can place the transparency on the tile as you're designing so you can see the proper placement of all of your elements. Once the paste is dry, brush on a layer of antiquing gel for a perfectly aged finish. When everything is dry, attach the transparency to the decorated tile and add any final touches to the top layer such as lace, photo anchors and popped up stickers.

technique tips

You can create a variety of embellishments for your scrapbook pages and cards with texture paste and other items you may already have in your scrapbooking stash. Try one of these ideas the next time you need a funky embellishment.

Apply a layer of texture paste to a chipboard tile. Use a comb or fork to create wavy designs in the paste and let dry. Lightly ink the edges of the tile and add a rub-on frame. Decorate with a chipboard letter covered in dimensional glaze and glitter glue (fig. 1).

Adhere a snowflake mask onto a chipboard tile and scrape a layer of texture paste. Remove the mask and let dry. Replace the mask and cover the texture paste with a layer of glitter glue (fig. 2).

Place a hollow chipboard circle onto a chipboard tile. Apply a layer of texture paste. Remove the circle and let dry. Add a brad to the center of the flower and rub-ons to the corners. Cover the cardstock center with

dimensional glaze and finally add drops of glitter glue to the circular rub-ons (fig. 3).

Trim a shape with a die-cutting system. Place the negative shape onto a chipboard tile and apply a layer of texture paste. Peel off the die-cut mask and let dry. Paint the heart with pearlescent paint and glitter. Once dry, cover the texture paste heart and outline with dimensional glaze (fig. 4).

fig. 1

fig. 2

fig. 4

fig. 3

A 3" (8cm) SQUARE of textured clay was the perfect mat for the front of this chipboard day planner. Air-dry clay is fun to use because it can be molded into almost any shape and colored into just about any shade of the rainbow. Roll a thin layer of clay, press into a textured template or other textured surface and peel off. Use a craft knife to trim the clay into the shape and size of your choosing. Allow 24 hours for the clay to dry so it is hard, but flexible. Once dry, paint, ink or attach brads to the clay.

yep, this is us first thing in the morning on any given Sunday.

Hair in a pony tail, still in jammies and not long out

of bed. I don't know why we decided to take this

photo that morning, but I'm glad we did so that we'll

always have this reminder of our favorite and most laid

back day of the week. One Sunday in April 2005

On Any Given Sunday

AIR-DRY CLAY BUTTONS ARE the perfect embellishments for layouts with a fun and playful tone. Roll out a thin layer of clay and press into a textured template or other textured surface. Use craft or kitchen cookie cutters to cut into fun shapes and let the clay dry completely. Color the clay with two coats of paint and a final layer of finishing glaze to add shine. Finally, add button holes either by hand or with an anywhere hole punch.

when I sit and think about my life, I can't believe that
I have lived in Canada for more than two thirds of it.

It feels like forever ago that I was 11 and my family
moved from England, but then just like yesterday all

at the same time. But no matter how long
I have been here, Canada is still not my

HOME

It's hard to explain what the heart feels.
I do like Canada, I have a good life,

lots of friends and opportunities, but
there is this hole in my heart, a void

that can't be filled. Some people tell me
to just move back there, but that's not

so easy now that I have Canadian born
children and I don't want them to feel

as I do. But every now and again that
hole is filled for a short while when I do

get to go back
home. Home to

ENGLAND

TRANSFER INK IS THE ideal medium for creating soft, watercolor-like images.
On this page the large transferred photograph was used in a similar way as
patterned paper. After transferring the photo onto cardstock (see step-by-step
instructions), use a ruler to tear straight edges around the photo to create a mat.
Sew the photograph onto the background paper and attach a printed transparency
on top to create an additional muted printed layer.

1 Print a photograph from an inkjet printer onto regular computer paper. (Remember when you transfer the photo, its mirror image will appear; print the photo in reverse if you want the original image). Place the photo face down on your cardstock.

2 Spray the back of the photograph with the transfer ink until the paper is saturated.

3 Apply even pressure by rolling a brayer across the back of the photo to transfer your image onto the cardstock.

4 Carefully peel back the original photo to reveal the image underneath. Re-spray with the transfer ink and apply pressure to any areas that did not completely transfer.

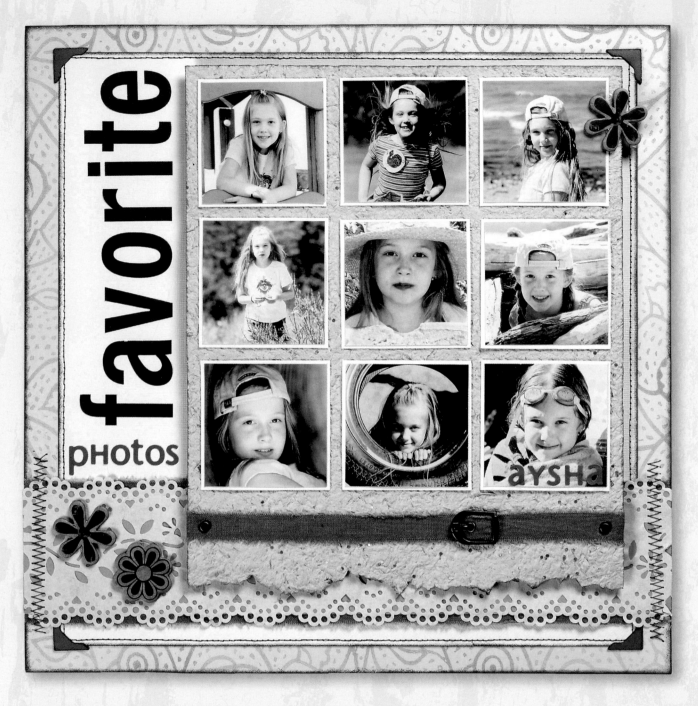

ALTHOUGH THERE ARE MANY beautiful handmade papers available for purchase, it is sometimes still fun to create and customize your own. To create a similar look as this layout, mix pink Paper Perfect with blue fibers and glitter to make an 8½" x 10" (22cm x 25cm) sheet (see step-by-step instructions). Once dry, trim, tear or die cut the handmade paper into any shape or size, and ink just as you would any other paper. If you want to raise the handmade paper with adhesive foam squares, adhere it to a sheet of chipboard so it is more stable and will not sag in the middle.

1 Scoop some Paper Perfect into a cup. Sprinkle in any glitter, fibers or dried flowers into the cup and mix with a palette knife.

2 Spread the mixture onto a page protector to the desired thickness. Sprinkle on any additions or press dried flowers into the spread mixture. Press down with the palette knife or fan brush. Let dry for 12-24 hours. (Drying time will vary depending on the thickness of your mixture.)

3 Once the mixture is dry, peel off from the page protector and cut, tear or die cut into the desired shape or layer onto your page.

FRIENDSHIP IS A SPECIAL GIFT

USE PAPER PERFECT TO do more than just make large sheets of paper to serve as backgrounds. To create this funky flower, spread the Paper Perfect mixture into the empty negative space of a chipboard flower circle. Let dry for 24 hours. Carefully push the flower shape out of the chipboard mold and then add to your scrapbook page or card.

Two beautiful Hyacinth Macaws.

We live in a major tourist town yet we hardly ever go and visit all of the attractions Victoria has to offer. Once we found out that the Crystal Gardens were going to close and the animals and birds relocated, we had to go and see it while we still had the chance.

The **birds** of Crystal Gardens

ALCOHOL INKS ARE ONE of my favorite types of colorants. Their vibrant colors and easy application (see step-by-step instructions) create stunning, one-of-a-kind effects. Combining two shades of orange ink with touches of fuchsia was the perfect choice for these funky patterned papers and stunning photographs. Apply alcohol ink to acid-free invisible tape to create ready-made adhesive strips that can be quickly adhered to your layout as a border or directional line.

These instructions show how to apply alcohol ink to transparent tape, but will work for application of any non-porous surface.

1 Lay a strip of transparent tape onto a sheet of tin foil or sheet protector (fold one end of the tape back so it will be easier to peel off later). Apply a few drops of blending solution onto a piece of felt or cotton ball and wipe it over the tape.

2 Secure a clean piece of felt onto the applicator tool and add a few drops of alcohol ink onto the felt. (I like to use two or three different colors.)

3 Dab the applicator tool onto the tape to transfer the ink. Don't rub or slide the applicator, as this will smear the colors. Peel off the tape and apply directly to your project. If you are not happy with the results, simply use some blending solution on a cotton ball to wipe clean and start the process over.

From everything we had heard, Hubbard Glacier was an amazing sight and people would be claiming their spots on the outside decks long before we would actually arrive there. Obviously that's all I needed to hear and we all got ourselves bundled up and outside to get a railing spot on the very front tip of the ship. We had several hours to wait and it was so bitterly cold. With the speed that the ship was moving along with the wind and rain we were soaking wet and frozen to the bone, but it was all worth it as the glacier was one of the most amazing sights we had ever seen.

Brr

September 19th, 2006

Photo: Phyllis Wright

CLEAR ACRYLIC SHAPES TAKE on an "icy" appearance when colored with cool tones of alcohol inks and silver and pearl mixatives. First, apply a layer of blue and green alcohol inks to the letters and photo anchors. Follow with a layer of the pearl and silver mixatives applied in the same manner as the inks. In this example, I decided to color the snowflakes with the mixatives only to maintain their clear icy look. Build your layout with wavy strips of embossed patterned papers and the acrylic shapes. Add random drops of silver glitter glue to put the final shimmering touch on a frosty layout.

The port at Costa Maya was beautiful, there were lots of little straw huts along a beautiful beach with clear blue waters. We disembarked the ship and walked into a market square where we had to find the meeting place for our excursion to the ruins of Kohunlich and Dzibanche. While we were waiting for everyone to arrive, there were some local people dressed in traditional Mayan clothing. They danced around the fountains playing their instruments and posed so all of the tourists could take photos. April '05

METALLIC LEAFING FLAKES ARE rich in color and provide an instant makeover to whatever they are applied to. The colorful gold-trimmed costumes of the Mayan dancers were perfectly accented with simple metallic strips resulting in little else being required to complete the page. To create the metallic strips, simply trim various widths of chipboard and apply an even layer of spray adhesive. Apply pieces of the metallic leafing sheets and press down firmly. Brush off any excess flakes. Finally, place the cardstock strips along the bottom of the page, adhering every other strip with dimensional foam squares.

Photo: Alex Sigurdson

CLEAR SCRAPBOOK FRAMES ARE an ideal canvas for creating dimensional wall art, and metallic leafing flakes are a perfect medium with which to embellish them. After creating the metallic leafing border (see step-by-step instructions), build the layout so it fits around what is on the top of the frame. Remember to place some of the page elements on foam squares to create a dimensional effect when combined with those on the frame. Once the layout is complete, finish the frame's design with the addition of chipboard letters and ribbon. Add black glitter glue to the letters and dimensional glaze to the metallic design.

1 Trim a piece of cardstock to 7 5/8" x 7 5/8" (19cm x 19cm). Position the mask along one side of the cardstock and trace with pencil. Trim along the edge of the mask leaving no less than a 1/8" (3mm) border of cardstock.

2 Use temporary adhesive to secure the larger piece of cardstock to the frame. Place the mask directly on the frame where it fits in the cut design. Be sure both pieces are securely adhered to the frame and spray with adhesive.

3 Remove the mask and cardstock and press metallic leafing flakes onto the adhesive. Rub with your finger to make sure it is firmly adhered.

4 Use a stiff, dry paintbrush to brush away any excess flakes and to reveal the design. (To antique the metallic flakes, replace the mask and rub the metallic flakes with a black inkpad and wipe with a tissue. You can also apply a layer of dimensional glaze for added shine.)

After a very rough ferry ride from Cozumel to Playa del Carmen we had to walk straight to the meeting place to catch the coach which would take us on our excursion through a Mexican jungle to some of the Mayan ruins.

After a very long and very hot day, we were dropped back off in Playa del Carmen and finally had the time to walk around this cute little town.

This really pleased Aysha as her main goal of the cruise was to shop....to shop as much as she possibly could. Who cares about ancient ruins when there are stores you can shop in? Plus she was dying to barter with the shopkeepers. So we stopped in every tacky T-shirt and souvenir shop there was....and all Aysha bought was snacks!

SHOPPING

MEXICAN STYLE

April 2005

NOTHING CREATES THAT TROPICAL feeling quite like batik fabrics. Using batik resist medium with foam stamps allows you to easily create the same look without having to use the messy traditional method of hot melted wax. After creating a batik design on fabric with colors similar to those in my photograph (see step-by-step instructions), I kept my page design and color scheme simple to maintain the light-hearted feel of the photo and to create continuity with the strong colors of the cute zebra statue.

1 Use a brush to paint a foam stamp with batik resist medium and stamp onto your fabric. Let the medium dry completely.

2 Dab, paint or spray the fabric with dye and let dry. (Because I was using a strong colored dye and I wanted my fabric to be lighter, I did not let my fabric dry completely). *Tip: I recommend using rubber gloves to protect your hands from being stained by the dye.*

3 Rinse the fabric in water to wash out all of the resist medium and any extra dye until you achieve the desired color. Let the fabric dry.

Erikia and I first met back in July 2003 when we were both teaching at Camp Memory Makers in Houston, Texas. I had a spare block and sat in on one of her classes. We would say "Hi" to each other as we passed each other in the hallways, but it wasn't until the following year that we were both teaching at CMM again and we started hanging out with each other that we really became friends. Being that I live in BC and Erikia lives in Colorado, we don't get to see each other much other than at trade shows and conventions, but we do keep in touch via email and I am proud to call her my friend. CMM Dearborn, Michigan 08/04

Photo: Torrey Scott

ONE OF MY FAVORITE things about this wonderful hobby is the ability to take an item and alter it in such a way that it is unique to my projects and personal taste. Adirondack washes allow you to dye fabrics, ribbons, laces and twills, resulting in beautiful shades and intensities of color. These washes are strong so I recommend dying your items in a kitchen or laundry room sink and wearing rubber gloves. First, dampen your item with water so it can better absorb the wash. Then simply spray or use an eyedropper to apply single or multiple colors to your item. For darker shades, simply let your item dry as is. For a medium shade, let it partially dry and then rinse in water. For a lighter shade, rinse with water right away and then let dry.

COMBINING RUB-ON IMAGES OR letters with Adirondack wash is a great way to make creative backgrounds for scrapbook pages and cards. First, apply a white rub-on to a white square of cotton fabric, and then dye with purple Adirondack wash. Next, spritz the fabric with water to create the subtle mottled background, and set aside to dry. The rub-on will work as a mask keeping the image white. Embellish with additional black rub-ons, glitter glue and a rhinestone brad to result in a beautiful all-occasion card.

THERE ARE SO MANY beautiful silk flowers available on the market. Dye them with Adirondack washes to turn them into one-of-a-kind blossoms that will beautifully enhance any project, such as this altered lunch box. After dampening the silk flowers, spray the centers with the wash and then use an eyedropper to drop water onto various parts of the flower to create the soft, mottled look. Add a metal washer and a rhinestone brad to the center and touches of glitter glue to the petals to complete the flower. Finally, dye torn fabric strips with two different colors of Adirondack wash, and tie them to the handle amongst a variety of ribbons.

forever

if only i could just

FREEZE

this moment in

♡ TIME

Straight grain of fabric

DATE: 84/06

aysha - promise
me you won't
grow up too
fast? take the
time to enjoy
your youth.

25 26 27 28 29 30 36

"WOOLCO"
THE VERY BEST
ENGLISH NEEDLES
PARTICULARLY SMOOTH

No 1
ALTERATIONS

paper 5

Patterned Paper

Handmade Paper

Watercolor Paper

Paper Piercing

Dry Embossing

Chipboard

Cardboard

Puffy Paper

Distressing

PAPER. THE BACKBONE OF our scrapbooks and the thing that makes our precious photos shine. Although we love the variety of embellishments available on the market, paper is the first thing many of us look for when checking out the aisles at our local scrapbooking store. With so many different types of paper, there is something for every mood and style. But there is so much more to paper than just pretty or funky patterns. There's a wide variety of types and textures with each sheet being a blank canvas just waiting for you to customize. Handmade papers can be beautiful and romantic or earthy and rugged; watercolor paper brings out your inner artist; and puffy paper helps you create just about any texture and page embellishment you can dream of.

So no matter what your preference in paper, it can easily be used to add visual and tactile texture to your scrapbook pages. Throughout the following chapter we will explore many different types of paper and learn how they can easily be altered to be so much more than just a foundation.

Patterned Paper

After our dog sledding excursion in Skagway we had some time to walk around the town and look in all of the shops and because we were so close to Russia, there was lots of Russian influences in the gifts and artwork that was for sale. I wasn't

really planning on buying much, if anything at all, but I kept on seeing these beautifully hand painted wooden Russian Father Frosts. I instantly fell in love with them and knew I had to have one. We found this one store that had the largest

collection and the best prices in town, the problem was that there were so many to choose from it was hard to decide. Finally I chose a medium sized red and blue one with copper accents and I loved it. But then we went into another store

and I saw this beautiful smaller one, so I just decided that I would like to start collecting them (though I should have chosen something cheaper and that I didn't have to travel so far to buy.) A few days later when we were in Ketchikan I

saw one that was sitting on a polar bear and thought it was quite different to the others that I had seen and picked that one up too. So this is how my little Father Frost collection started, and I only hope I have the chance to add more to it.

father frost

Alaska trip: September 17th – 24th, 2006
Journaling and photo: October 29th, 2006

IF I WERE TO list my top five favorite scrapbooking items, patterned papers would surely make the cut. The colors, styles and patterns are endless, and, thankfully, manufacturers never run out of beautiful new styles for us to fall in love with. When layering different patterns, I find they can often blend into each other a bit too much and appear lost. Simply inking around the edges makes the layers "pop" and adds more depth. Glitter glues also add a perfect touch to customize your papers. Simply add random drops to create a look all your own.

technique tips

There are many different things you can do with patterned paper to personalize your projects. Whether you use one technique or combine several, the results are sure to please.

Trim designs from the patterned paper and adhere strips of wire to the back so you can shape your design. Trim additional pieces of the pattern, and layer with dimensional foam adhesive.

Use decorative scissors to trim strips of paper and fold to create pleats. Machine sew the pleats flat and add a second strip of patterned paper with dimensional foam adhesive to cover the stitching.

Many computer fonts are outlines rather than solid letters. These fonts work perfectly (as do many dingbat fonts) for printing on patterned papers to create custom lettering and other designs such as the patterned letters and arrow in this example.

ONE GREAT THING ABOUT paper is it can be trimmed into any shape. I recommend using cutting templates to make intricate-looking patterns a cinch. Use a temporary adhesive to secure your template onto the patterned paper, and use the template's cutting groves to cut the design into your paper with a fine-tipped craft knife. Remove the template and fold the paper flaps back to reveal the white reverse side of the paper. Add drops of glitter glue to the white cardstock for the finishing touch. This technique works perfectly for cards and scrapbook pages alike, and with so many double-sided papers on the market, the design possibilities are endless!

I LOVE UNFINISHED BOOKS—their blank covers just begging to be transformed into the perfect album. To create this cover, trim a piece of cardstock the same size as the front of the book. This not only provides the papers more stability when sewing them together, it is also much easier to work on a flat surface and adhere it to the album's cover when finished. After combining various patterned papers for the foundation, trim flowers from another coordinating sheet. Add mini brads, glitter glue and dimensional glaze for a touch of texture and personality to finish off a custom-covered album.

WITH THE WIDE VARIETY of handmade and specialty papers available there is something for every style. When conceptualizing this page, I knew I wanted to have a romantic, vintage feel. The deep textures in the cream handmade paper worked well with the textured creases in the muslin flower, and also made it easy for me to stamp the page's subtitle. Notice how I left the chipboard photo corners uncovered; not all chipboard needs to be covered, and my choice for leaving these au naturel worked perfectly with the other elements on the page.

Thankful. That's what I am on this Thanksgiving day. Thankful that we've had another year with Tia. Now at 12½ years old, she is a senior citizen as far as dogs go and we certainly see it in her behavior. She's definitely slowed down and doesn't run around like she use to, but her sweet, loving nature is still the same and we'll just love her and spend time with her while we can....and be thankful for every moment we have. October 8th, 2006

thankful

Photo: Aysha Sigurdson

SPECIALTY PAPERS COME IN a wide variety of textures, from satiny smooth to deeply wrinkled, and everything in between. Working with them can often be intimidating, but it doesn't have to be. Just as you have to provide balance when mixing patterned papers by using a small, medium and large scale of pattern, the same principle applies when combining specialty (textured) papers. On this page, you will notice the mint paper has a subtle linen texture, the lavender paper has a medium texture with wrinkles and flakes of mica, and the silver paper has the heaviest, most defined texture. Remember to keep all elements proportional and the result will be a visually balanced and eye-pleasing page.

May you never lose

RaCHeL

your sense of wo...

YOU DON'T NEED TO be an artist to incorporate watercolor paper into your scrapbooks. All you need is some dye inks, plastic wrap and watercolor paper (see step-by-step instructions). After creating your custom-made watercolor paper, select a background that really makes your colors "pop." I found that black worked best for this example. To create even more texture and interest to a solid background, trim the cardstock into random squares and rectangles, and sew them to another sheet of cardstock. Finally, add white glitter chipboard embellishments to brighten the page and add a touch of youthful whimsy.

1 Use masking tape to secure a piece of watercolor paper to a wooden board or the back of a cookie sheet.

2 After dampening the paper with water, spray with Adirondack wash or dye. For more interesting designs, use several different colors.

For this technique, I recommend using rubber gloves to protect your hands from being stained by the dye.

3 Cover the watercolor paper with plastic wrap. As the wrap clings to the damp paper, gently maneuver it with your fingers to create pockets and veins of dye for variations in color and intensity.

4 Let the paper dry completely before removing the plastic wrap.

Paris

The Paris Hotel and Casino is such an impressive sight and the view from the top is amazing, especially at night when you can see the Vegas lights for miles and miles. Now I just want to see the real tower. January 2003

MANY CRAFTERS HAVE AT least one, if not more, anywhere hole punches in their stash of scrapbooking tools. You many not be aware of it, but these punches have more creative uses than simply setting eyelets and attaching brads. Creating a negative image design with various-sized punches (see step-by-step instructions) allows you to create the perfect page element while keeping your page clean and simple. This easy technique will enhance the visual textures in your photographs, and allow them to remain the focus of the layout.

1 Draw a shape or design on a piece of card-stock with a pencil. If you're not comfort-able drawing by hand, use a template or trace around a chipboard shape as shown here.

2 Use various-sized anywhere hole punches to create a design along the pencil lines. Erase the pencil lines.

3 Trim pieces of cardstock or patterned papers to fit behind the holes, and attach to the back of your layout. Use one color of cardstock as shown here, or use a variety of colors as shown on the opposite page. Use glitter glue or dimensional glaze to add extra effects, if desired.

Piglet has always been one of our favorite Disney characters but in all the times that we have been to Disneyland, we have never seen him. Maybe this trip to DisneyWorld would be different, maybe we would finally get to see him there. We soon learnt that all of the 100 Acre Wood characters lived in the Animal Kingdom...but we didn't see Piglet. We saw a double decker bus full of characters in Epcot Center...but no Piglet. Where was he? Why could we never see him? On our last day I waited for about an hour to watch the 'Share A Dream Come True' parade while the kids decided to go on the rides instead. Finally about half way through the parade there he was, the elusive Piglet...and both of the kids missed it.

think
PiNK

November 11th 2004

DESIGNS CREATED WITH ANYWHERE hole punches don't always have to be classic and sophisticated. They can also be playful and fun, as shown in this example. After creating the bulk of your page, use the negative space left over from a package of chipboard to trace the flourish designs, and back the holes with various colored sheets of cardstock. To balance the design, add various-sized holes to the left corners of the photograph. Finally, add random drops of glitter glue to some of the holes to finish off this fun, whimsical layout.

Alex and Richard
Thanksgiving Dinner, October 8th, 2006

Having most of my family live half a world way makes me treasure the ones who live near by all the more. Rich is my second cousin and since the kids and I moved to Victoria 8 years ago we have become much closer and rather than a cousin type of relationship, Rich and Libby are much more like a third set of grandparents to the kids.

USE SOME OF THE chipboard shapes in your scrapbooking stash to add a modern twist to dry embossing. Begin by adhering chipboard stars (or any shape of your choosing) to the *back* of a strip of patterned cardstock that has a white core. Use a spoon to rub the *front* of the cardstock to find the edges of the stars. Once you know where the shapes are, use an embossing stylus to trace around the stars to create the raised design. Lightly sand the stars to highlight the design. This will result in a border that perfectly plays up the other patterned papers and chipboard shapes on the page. Finally, add subtle embossed lines on the plaid patterned circle with the scoring blade on your paper trimmer.

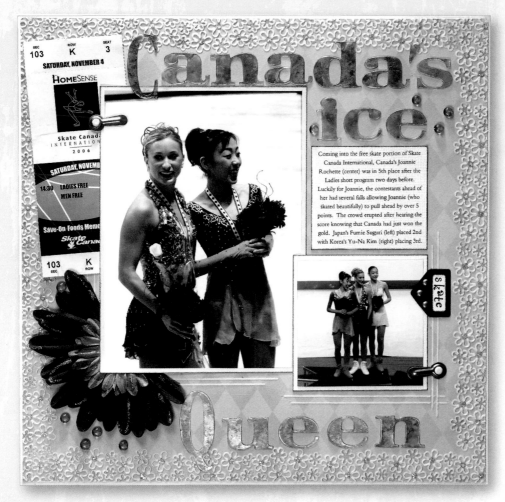

Canada's Ice Queen

Coming into the free skate portion of Skate Canada International, Canada's Joannie Rochette (center) was in 5th place after the Ladies short program two days before. Luckily for Joannie, the contestants ahead of her had several falls allowing Joannie (who skated beautifully) to pull ahead by over 5 points. The crowd erupted after hearing the score knowing that Canada had just won the gold. Japan's Fumie Suguri (left) placed 2nd with Korea's Yu-Na Kim (right) placing 3rd.

MANY DIE-CUTTING SYSTEMS HAVE embossing dies that are perfect for creating intricate or large area designs like my example shown here. Create an embossed border (see step-by-step instructions) and design the remainder of your page. Use the scoring blade on your paper trimmer to create embossed lines (which can be lightly sanded) around your photographs. As a final touch, add drops of silver glitter glue to each of the small flowers and dimensional iridescent glitter glue to the centers of each of the large flowers to play up the page's "icy" theme.

1 Sand around the front edges of a 12" X 12" (30cm x 30cm) square piece of cardstock with a white core. On the opposite side, measure 1¼" (3cm) in from the edge of each side, and draw a pencil line on all four sides.

2 Use an embossing die to line up the top edge of the die with the pencil line, and squeeze the tool. Emboss the design all around the edge of the cardstock.

3 Sand the embossed border on the front of the cardstock to highlight the embossed image. To bring extra detail to the embossed design, add dimensional glaze or glitter glue to various parts of the image.

Chipboard

CHIPBOARD IS DEFINITELY ON my "Top 5" list of favorite scrapbooking products. It is so versatile and can work for any theme or style of paper crafting. For this 6" x 6" (15cm x 15cm) square mini tribute album, the chipboard covers were a perfect canvas for embellishment. Adhere chipboard letters to the cover of the album and apply several coats of white paint to the entire surface. Once dry, sand the edges of the album and the letters, and attach the die-cut chipboard strips (see step-by-step instructions). Apply two coats of varnish to protect and seal the cover. Add a silk flower, highlight with glitter glue and attach the distressed chipboard number to the center. If the varnish has a matte satin finish, cover the chipboard letters and numeral "4" with a layer of dimensional glaze.

technique tips

Add additional designs to your chipboard strip with various-sized anywhere hole punches or slot punch tools.

1 Remove the ejection foam from the die. Secure a chipboard strip to the die with a temporary adhesive to keep the strip centered while cutting.

2 Place the chipboard and die into the tool and gently squeeze. Don't press too hard—you only want to cut through the top layers of chipboard.

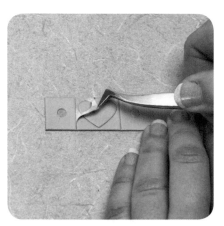

3 Remove the die and chipboard and use tweezers to peel off the top colored layer of chipboard, removing the negative space of the die's image.

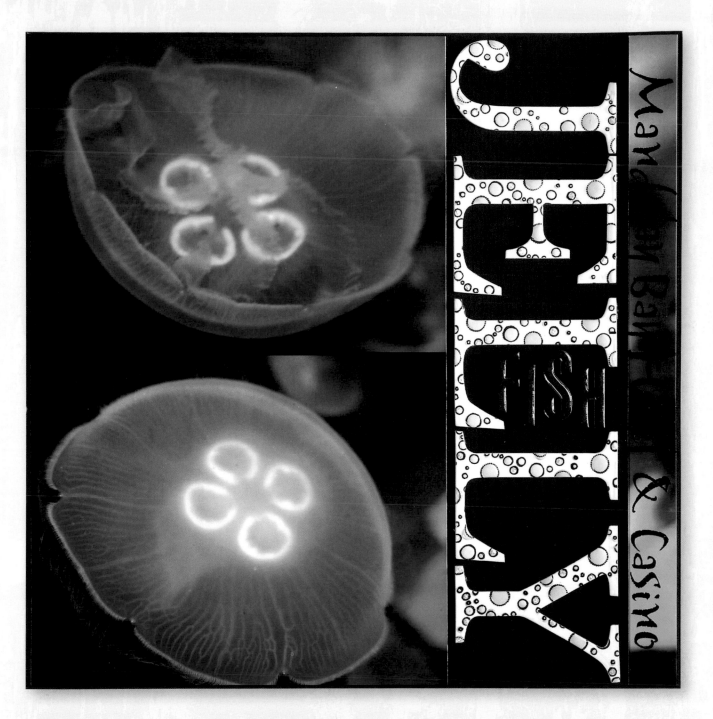

WITH SUCH STRONG AND impactive photographs, I wanted to keep my page elements to a minimum in this example. Large chipboard letters will allow you to add a bit of design and interest while keeping things simple. To play up on the shapes in your photographs, stamp various circles on the letters and then fill with either clear or blue dimensional glaze and dimensional glitter glue. To complete the title, color smaller chipboard letters with blue stamping ink and then finish with a layer of clear dimensional glaze.

May your sand castles never fall,
May your piers stand strong;

May your waves crash gently, and your beaches be long,
May your waters be clear, may your pails be light.

May your breezes be warm, and your sun be bright,
Wherever you go, whatever you do,

May you always take the wonders
of the beach with you.

- Brandie Valenzuela

Alex, you are PURE JOY

Alex at Willows Beach, Oak Bay
April 21st, 2006

CORRUGATED CARDBOARD IS A great way to add visual and tactile texture to your pages. It's inexpensive, readily available and the perfect item to bring out some of the rougher textures from your photographs. Use this surface as a mat to bring extra focus to a smaller photograph and to provide visual balance with items anchored along the bottom border of the page. If you thread twine through the corrugated ridges of the cardboard strip and wrap the top of the strip with twine, it will lie flat on the page, reducing any additional bulk.

CORRUGATED CARDBOARD CAN ALSO be used to create rugged foundations for cute page or album cover embellishments. Peel the majority of the top layer of cardboard from a piece of corrugated cardboard and distress the edges by roughing them up with the edge of a pair of scissors. Ink a pre-made chipboard photo mat and attach to the corrugated cardboard. Add further embellishment with a coordinating chipboard sticker, brads, twine and a metal paper clip.

fig. 1   *fig. 2*   *fig. 3*

IF YOU'RE LOOKING FOR a unique way to dress up a Christmas card, try using a painted piece of corrugated cardboard cut into an elongated triangle to work as a Christmas tree. Add further charm with a ribbon "trunk," jeweled "lights" and a micro bead star to complete the look with contrasting textures.

technique tips

Depending on the look you are trying to achieve, you may want to remove part or the entire top layer of cardboard from a piece of corrugated cardboard. Simply peel the top layer if you want the majority of it to still be attached to the base (fig. 1). Spray the top layer with water to soften the cardboard to let you remove a larger slice of it (fig. 2). Spray the top layer with water and let it sit for awhile to soften it even more. You can then peel off most, if not all, of the top layer (fig. 3).

Aysha

After our tour around GatorPark in the morning, we took a taxi out to the famous South Beach area of Miami. The beach was beautiful and with it's aqua blue waters and soft white sand, so very different from the rocky beaches we have at home. Even the wind didn't stop people from laying on the sand or Aysha taking a dip in the Atlantic Ocean. Nov '04

South Beach
Florida

PUFFY PAPER IS A fun and photo-safe way to bring just about any texture to your scrapbook and other paper craft projects. Simply trim it with a craft knife into any shape, and then texturize by firmly pressing rubber stamps, textured templates (as I used in this example), or any other textured item into its surface. If you prefer a smooth surface, simply leave as is. Whether you choose a textured or flat surface, add an additional touch of playful sparkle with random drops of glitter glue to make it shimmer and shine.

Just

chillin'

This is a typical sight at any time around our house. Alex glued to some sort of video game and Aysha listening to her music.

On this particular day we had gone to Libby and Rich's for a BBQ as Hazel and John had come out from England for a couple of weeks.

The kids were not particularly interested in listening to what us adults were talking about and decided to sit in the shade and tune out.

That's all right, because at least while they are doing this it means that for once they aren't fighting with each other!
July 30th, 2006

PUFFY PAPER IS AVAILABLE in both black and white, but you can easily paint it to match the color scheme of your layout. Use layers of embossed and glittered patterned papers to create the foundation for your page. Attach photographs with dimensional foam adhesive to make them "pop" off the page. Use the puffy paper brackets (see step-by-step instructions) to frame the photographs. You can easily attach them to the page with dimensional foam adhesive.

1 Place the chipboard bracket onto the puffy paper. Using a craft knife, trim around the outline of the shape.

2 Press the trimmed shapes firmly into a textured surface to create the impression. Press firmly with your hands for small shapes. Use a rolling pin or brayer to create deeper impressions for larger shapes.

3 Add a layer of silver paint to the textured side of the puffy paper. Once dry, rub the surface with black ink to further highlight the texture. Add a layer of dimensional glaze to finish.

Distressing

I LOVE THE LOOK that can be achieved when you take something clean and new, and distress it so it looks like a family heirloom that has been passed down through the generations. I used several distress techniques to create the finished look on this frame. Ink patterned papers and scrape the edges with a distress tool. Dye embellishments (in this case the flash card, muslin flower and strips) with walnut ink crystals. Dye the chipboard flourishes with a walnut ink dauber and chalk ink. The dauber will dampen the chipboard, allowing you to work the edges so they will peel to look more weathered. Once all the elements are combined, the result is a wonderful vintage photo clipboard.

technique tips

Walnut stain ink is one of my favorite items to use to distress and age different elements on scrapbook pages. These tags show a variety of techniques that will achieve a variety of looks.

Dip the tag in the ink once for a slightly aged look. Let dry, then dip a second time for a darker shade (fig. 1).

Sprinkle the tag with salt to absorb the ink to create interesting patterns (brush off the salt once dry). Or, ink the tag so it is quite wet and cover with plastic wrap (fig. 2). See the watercolor technique on page 91 for detailed instructions.

Paint the tag with ink, let partially dry, and then spray with water or additional ink. Notice how the ink or water blends to create soft mottled patterns (fig. 3).

Mix beverage crystals or food coloring with the ink for different colors. Here I used lime-flavored crystals to create a vintage olive shade and cherry-flavored crystals to create a vintage red shade (fig. 4).

dipped once · double dipped · salt · plastic wrap

fig. 1 · *fig. 2*

Painted and sprayed with water · Painted and sprayed with ink · green koolaid · red kool aid

fig. 3 · *fig. 4*

gypsies

6/11/02

Coming from England, seeing gypsies and their caravans

in the countryside is not an uncommon sight (though that

is certainly not the case in Canada). We had gone with

Uncle Colin and Aunty Marm for a drive and came across

an authentic gypsy caravan. Not knowing that gypsies were actually real, the kids were so surprised to see it and wanted to stop for

me to take a photo. Well, we all knew that this would not be taken too kindly by the owner if they were to see us do this

Uncle Colin drove up and down the road a couple of times so I could discreetly take pictures out of the car window.

Near Bibury in the Cotswolds, Gloucestershire, England

THIS DISTRESSED CARDSTOCK LOOKS as if it would have taken hours to create, but it only took about ten minutes. Begin by inking the edges of your cardstock with distress ink, and then scrunch it into a ball to add creases and wrinkles. Lay flat and rub the surface with antique linen, vintage photo and walnut stain shades of distress ink. *(Tip: start with the lightest shade of ink so you don't transfer any of the darker ink onto the lighter ink pad.)* Spray the cardstock with water to blend the colors, and then iron to flatten and dry. Spritz the cardstock with walnut stain ink and iron again to dry. Lightly rub the cardstock with vintage photo ink to highlight some of the wrinkles. Follow these easy steps and you will create a beautifully distressed, ready-to-use piece of cardstock.

A little girl is one of the most beautiful miracles of life. - Unknown

emily

Sitting

Pretty @

clear elements

Beads

Sequins

Transparencies

Acrylics

Shrink Plastic

Glass

WHEN THINKING OF TEXTURE, clear elements are probably not one of the first things that come to mind. But when you think about it, not everything clear is smooth and…well…clear. Glass can be completely clear and flat, or frosted with an interesting "pebbled" texture. Calm ocean water can look like ripples of silk gently blowing in the breeze, or rough and jagged as waves crash against a rocky coastline. The clear elements we incorporate into our albums and paper crafts can vary equally as much as those found in nature, and although we might instantly associate them with page themes of water, snow or ice (which they are perfect for), you will soon see here that they work equally well with many other page topics. Knowing that nothing ruins a layout like visible and unsightly adhesive, many crafters struggle with how to adhere these tricky items to their pages. So along with learning some of my favorite techniques for using clear products, you'll find successful ways to attach them as well.

As you read through this final chapter of *Tantalizing Textures*, clear your mind as you learn how to add creative touches and express your inner artist while clearly adding more texture than originally thought possible with this versatile medium. I'll show you how to alter and layer a variety of clear elements with techniques that can easily be applied to paper crafting and scrapbooking.

I have known Karen for about 8 years and not only is she a great friend, but she is also a great person. When we met I was at the lowest point in my life. Brett and I had just separated and the kids and I had moved to a new city, all in the same week.

Sensing that I might be in need of a friend, Karen knocked on my door

and invited the kids and I to her daughter's birthday party. Her

simple kind gesture of reaching out to me meant so much and we became

good friends. This is no surprise since Karen is one of the most warm

hearted people I know. She is a fantastic mother to her 3 girls and

is always there to help anyone any time she can. I feel so lucky to have her in my life and to be able to call her a friend.

08/05

Karen and Jenna

[One true friend] karen

WHEN YOU THINK OF adding beads to your scrapbooks you probably envision tediously sewing or adhering them to your layout one by one. Fortunately, you can purchase seed, bugle and micro beads mixed with clear drying adhesive that are easily applied to paper. Due to the playful nature of the papers and glittery embellishments, this title created with beads (see step-by-step instructions) and chipboard hearts covered with micro beads provides the perfect finishing touch.

1 Adhere the chipboard letter outline to a piece of cardstock.

2 Use a small spoon or scoop to spread the beads into the negative space of the chipboard letter. Let dry.

3 Once the bead mixture is dry, cover both the chipboard letter and beads with a layer of dimensional glaze.

technique tips

Here are some fun ways to incorporate beads onto your scrapbook and paper craft projects:

Create funky micro bead lettering by die cutting an adhesive sheet and covering with beads (fig. 1).

Create a framed micro bead mat to add some class to your lettering (fig. 2).

Hand sew beads to a painted chipboard shape and cover with a layer of dimensional glaze (fig. 3).

Create wire shapes decorated with beads (fig. 4). Many patterns and instructions can be found online or better yet, let your creativity take over and create your own!

fig. 1

fig. 2

fig. 3

fig. 4

I KEPT THE PAGE design of this layout relatively simple to allow the large photograph to be the focal point. Place your photo slightly higher on the page and stitch rows of sequins in the borders to add just the right amount of detail. Mix in a few heart sequins to provide extra personality and to reinforce the page theme.

108

YOU MAKE MY HeART...

Aysha and Tia

My two girls

October 2006

smile

LARGE FUNKY FLOWER SEQUINS are great to use on fun and youthful pages like this one. Although sequins add a lot of pizzazz on their own, it can also be fun to spice them up a bit. After adhering all of the decorative elements to your page, apply a variety of glitter glue and liquid pearls onto the sequins. Another fun way to create a quick and easy custom-made embellishment is to apply doodle-style rub-ons to a patterned paper shape such as this arrow.

WE OFTEN CONSTRUCT OUR page foundations with layers upon layers of patterned paper, but I recently discovered layered transparencies can provide the same striking visual effect. To create a unique background, add layers of inked transparencies between strips of patterned paper borders. Run a few pieces of transparency through a paper crimper to create further interest. Then ink this texture for more definition. Machine sewing, rub-on corners and chipboard hearts can provide more interest and a touch of color to a monotone background.

It doesn't matter how old you are, there is just something about walking

through the front gates of a Disney theme park that makes us all believers . . .

. . . even if it's only for the few hours you're there. Alex and Tigger Disney World - Nov '04

always believe

Warm Winter Wishes

TRANSPARENCIES HAVE MORE CREATIVE options than basic printing and stamping. For a fun idea, use the embossing dies from a die-cutting system to emboss a design onto a transparency backdrop. And just like on paper, you can sand the image with sandpaper to bring out the embossed design.

Eight time Canadian and 1987 world champion figure skater, Brian Orser, has always been one of my favorite skaters. I had been fortunate enough to see him skate live on several occasions and was in awe of his strong technical skills (his jumps were amazing!) . So imagine my thrill when in between coaching a couple of the skaters he was sat right in front of Dad and I while at the men's and ladies's finals of Skate Canada, and that he was gracious enough to pose for a photo with me . Skate Canada International at the Save-On-Foods Memorial Center, Victoria, B.C.

Meeting BRian

Photo: Roy Wright

ALTHOUGH THERE ARE MANY beautiful pre-printed transparencies on the market, it can be fun to create your own custom sheets to perfectly match your layouts. This paisley transparency was so easy to create. Simply scan a piece of your favorite patterned paper, change the color mode on your scanner to "black and white," and print onto a sheet of transparency. When combined on the layout with the matching patterned paper, the result is a completely cohesive design. To further customize the transparency, apply clear dimensional glaze to fill in some of the designs (like the paisleys) to create a unique epoxy look.

ACRYLIC ITEMS NOT ONLY work well for decorating cards and scrapbook pages, they can also be used to enhance album covers where their clear properties can be utilized to their full potential. The clear "floating" acrylic mat on the cover of this landscape album provides a unique look and is remarkably easy to create (see step-by-step instructions). Embellish with photo anchors, an index tab and silk flowers to create a truly beautiful cover.

1 Place an acrylic frame on the cover of a chipboard album, and trace around the outside and inside edges. Using a craft knife and a ruler, trim the frame. (Save the center of the frame to mat the photograph.)

2 Apply fuzzy (or traditional) rub-ons to the acrylic frame.

3 Trim a piece of transparency larger than the cut-out window. Adhere the transparency to the back of the cut-out so it covers the opening. Attach the acrylic frame to the front of the album. Add the photo mat to the center of the frame with adhesive dots hidden behind the rub-ons. Finish with a few drops of glitter glue over the paisley design.

COLORFUL ACRYLIC BUTTONS AND charms provide the perfect embellishments for this sweet picture frame. When attaching clear elements, a white base is usually best for blending in and hiding adhesive, however it is sometimes still visible. Apply a thin and even layer of liquid adhesive to minimize this risk, and be sure there are no air bubbles (these will show once the adhesive is dry). Another idea is to play up acrylic letters with etched designs. Cover the letters with ink and then wipe them clean. The ink will remain in the recessed areas of the etched designs.

Photo: Phyllis Wright

FUNKY FLOWERS AND DOODLE-STYLE papers were the perfect choice to pair with this adorable photo of my friend's daughter. To give acrylic letters more personality, emboss them with embossing templates from a die-cutting system. Blot the letters with solvent ink to further enhance the design. Give basic acrylic flowers a funky face lift by doodling around the edges and adding polka dots with dimensional paint. Add pearl brads to create striking centers and to discreetly adhere the acrylic flowers to your page.

Photo: Marcy O'Keefe

Aysha, Grandpa and Alex

Unfortunately I never had the chance to know either of my grandfathers, so that's why I am so glad that my kids not only know my dad, but are close to him. They may not realize how lucky they are now, but I know they will once they are older.

GOTTA [Love] grandpa

HAVING NOT PLAYED WITH shrink plastic since I was a child, I forgot how much fun it is to peek through the oven window and watch the transformation take place before my eyes. The oversized photo anchors and brackets I used on this project are so easy to create. Simply draw super-sized anchors on the plastic shrink sheet with a black marker, and use a large rubber stamp and solvent ink to create the brackets. Once your images are on the shrink plastic, simply trim and heat in the oven at 325°F for a few minutes (keeping a watchful eye). With this technique, you'll have ultra-cute page embellishments in no time!

technique tips

Here are a few more fun ideas for incorporating shrink plastic into your designs.

Draw or print dingbat shapes to create funky centers for silk flowers (fig. 1).

Trace around chipboard shapes, fill with color and add a design with rubber stamps (fig. 2); add funky curls of wire (fig. 3); layer on a second shrink plastic shape after the original shape has been shrunk (fig. 4).

Print or draw out title boxes and shrink. Add rub-on words and flowers, and embellish with liquid pearl and rhinestones (fig. 5).

Draw funky flowers and shrink. Fill the center of the flower with micro beads. Add a doodle-style rub-on and cover with a layer of dimensional glaze (fig. 6).

Stamp a border image along a strip of shrink plastic. Trim the strip with decorative scissors, punch holes along the scalloped edge and shrink (fig. 7).

fig. 1
fig. 2
fig. 3
fig. 4
fig. 5
fig. 6
fig. 7

TITLE LETTERS ARE AN ideal embellishment to create from shrink plastic and with the multitude of fonts available, the possibilities are endless. After shrinking the circular letters, paint the backs white so they will stand out against the blue patterned paper that slightly shows through and distorts the shrink plastic's natural color. Add a polished look to the doodle star background by adding silver glitter glue to some of the outline stars and black glitter glue to the black stars. Simple touches such as this add the "wow" factor to your scrapbook pages.

SUPER-CUTE EMBELLISHMENTS PERFECT FOR cards and scrapbook pages are easy to make with dingbat images from your computer. Since the finished size of your image will be about a quarter of the original size, be sure to enlarge your original image accordingly. Before you print onto your shrink plastic sheet, change your printer's paper setting to "Transparency" so less ink is used. Too much ink left sitting on the surface can take quite a while to dry and can bleed and distort your image. You can color your images before or after shrinking (I prefer to do it before because it is easier to color the larger image and your colors will intensify once shrunk). Add a touch of glitter glue to perfectly finish off these adorable little tiles.

LAYOUTS FEATURING LARGE PHOTOGRAPHS have strong visual impact and are also quick and easy to create. But that doesn't mean you can't add some creative and textural touches. To coordinate with the horizontal strips of patterned papers, create a strip of glass microscope slides and secure a snowflake mask on top. Apply aqua and silver alcohol inks over the mask. Remove the mask to reveal the snowflake design. To add an additional icy touch, apply silver glitter glue to the snowflakes. Finally, adhere the slides with a few drops of liquid adhesive to a strip of white cardstock, and attach to your page. *Tip: The mottled pattern of the microscope slides makes hiding the adhesive a snap since it blends in with the design.*

Aysha and Alex in Georgetown, Grand Cayman Islands

April 2005

OK, so you both say that you don't like each other (which I don't believe for one second), but since we are on holiday and having a good time can you pleeeease, just for one quick second, sit next to each other, give each other a hug and pretend that you like each other, just to make me happy so I can get a photo? Please?

Please Just
Pretend

WHEN I LOOK AT these pictures and remember our trip to the Cayman Islands, I think of how the ocean water was the clearest, most beautiful shade of aqua. Although this page's theme is not about the water, I still wanted it to be represented on the layout. Waves of mini aqua page pebbles (see step-by-step instructions) are the perfect way to incorporate this fond memory onto my layout.

1 Use a temporary adhesive to secure a piece of transparency to the negative space of a die-cut or chipboard shape.

2 Adhere mini glass pebbles along the pattern, filling in the negative space. Liquid adhesive doesn't dry as quickly on transparency, so be sure to allow sufficient drying time.

3 Remove the transparency from the die-cut sheet and trim around the glass-pebble image. Adhere to your page by applying adhesive under the pebbles.

supply lists

FERNY 10
Supplies: Patterned papers (My Mind's Eye); chipboard letters (Zsiage); brads, photo anchors, tape measure twill (Creative Impressions); lace (Rusty Pickle); decorative trims (BasicGrey); boarder rub-on, flower stamp (Adorn It); postmark rub-on, walnut ink crystals (7 Gypsies); die-cut tag (QuicKutz); pin (Making Memories); hook and eyes (Elan); floss (DMC); pattern (McCall's); distress ink (Ranger); adhesive foam (Therm O Web); buttons (unknown); safety pin; string; P22 Typewriter font (Internet download)

LOVE CARD 11
Supplies: Cardstock (Bazzill); metal tag, patterned paper (K&Co.); jump ring, safety pin, stickpins (Making Memories); buttons, muslin (unknown); walnut ink crystals (7 Gypsies); thread; adhesive foam (Therm O Web)

THE SHAWS 11
Supplies: Cardstock (Bazzill); chipboard letters (Li'l Davis); rub-on letters (American Crafts); walnut ink (7 Gypsies); stick pins (Making Memories); die-cut tag (QuicKutz); button hole twill (Adorn It); letter stamps (PSX); decorative trip (Me & My Big Ideas); brads (Creative Impressions); chalk ink (Clearsnap); distress ink (Ranger); adhesive tape (Therm O Web); liquid adhesive (Magic Scraps); ornate buckle (Elan); pattern (McCall's); Aida cloth; hooks and eyes; lace; needles; snaps

LITTLE MISS JENNA 12
Supplies: Patterned papers (EK Success); cardstock (Bazzill, Chatterbox); chipboard flowers (Maya Road); chipboard letters (Scenic Route); chipboard hearts (Making Memories); rub-on letters (Imagination Project); fabric strips (Maisy Mo); brads, photo anchors (Creative Impressions); die-cut index tab, photo corners, tag accents (QuicKutz); date stamp (Just Rite); dimensional glaze (Plaid); distress ink (Ranger); chalk ink (Clearsnap); adhesives (Therm O Web); FG Adam font (Font Garden)

MEMORIES FRAME 13
Supplies: Frame (Melissa Frances); cardstock (Bazzill); ribbon (American Crafts); solid green fabric strips (Maisy Mo); brads, rickrack (Creative Impressions); flower (Petaloo); chipboard word (Li'l Davis); rub-on letters (Adorn It); glitter glue (Ranger); jewels (Heidi Swapp); pink paper (Keeping Memories Alive); adhesives (Therm O Web)

JUST ME 13
Supplies: Cardstock; pink fabric (Wimpole Street Creations); chipboard letters (Heidi Swapp, Zsiage); die-cut letters and numbers (QuicKutz); metal photo corner (Scrapworks); chipboard flower (Li'l Davis); rub-on circles (Maisy Mo); dimensional glaze, pink and silver liquid pearl paints (Ranger); green paint (Making Memories); twill (Adorn It); brads, velvet trim (Creative Impressions); chalk ink (Clearsnap); acrylic heart (Heidi Grace); daisy trim, fabric, lace (unknown); jump ring; safety pin; adhesives (EK Success, Magic Scraps, Xyron); Tiempo font (Internet download)

IT'S THAT LOOK AGAIN 14
Supplies: Patterned paper (Chatterbox); ribbon (BasicGrey, May Arts, Textured Trios); rhinestone brads (SEI); other brads (Bazzill, Creative Impressions); flash card, photo anchors (7 Gypsies); die-cut index tab, jewelry tag (QuicKutz); distress ink (Ranger); chalk ink (Clearsnap); rub-on letters (Polar Bear Press); letter stamps (PSX); mini page pebbles (Memories in the Making); adhesive (Magic Scraps, Therm O Web); lace; staples

MONSTER MOGS 15
Supplies: Patterned papers, tag (We R Memory Keepers); letter stamps (Gel-a-tins); date stamp (Just Rite); rub-on accents, walnut ink crystals (7 Gypsies); metal index tab (Daisy D's); photo turns (Creative Impressions); brads (Bazzill); ribbon (American Crafts, Creative Impressions, Textured Trios); picture hooks (Li'l Davis); ink (Ranger, Tsukineko); sepia dimensional glaze (Plaid); adhesives (Therm O Web)

technique tip 15
Supplies: Ribbon (Textured Trios); walnut ink (7 Gypsies); dye (Making Memories); fiber (EK Success); adhesive (Therm O Web); beads; lace; thread

ANNIE BANANNIE 16
Supplies: Cardstock (Bazzill); chipboard letters (Li'l Davis); chipboard flowers (Everlasting Keepsakes); die-cut letters (QuicKutz); letter stamps (Hero Arts); ribbons (American Crafts, Heidi Grace, May Arts, Michaels); rub-on flowers (Maisy Mo); charm (Heidi Grace); mini page pebbles (Memories in the Making); dimensional glaze, distress ink, glitter glue (Ranger); chalk ink (Clearsnap); paint (Making Memories); adhesives (Therm O Web, Xyron); jump ring

LOVE YOU 17
Supplies: Cardstock, chipboard, heart stencil (Bazzill); ribbon (American Crafts); rickrack (Creative Impressions); chipboard letters (Heidi Swapp); letter stamps (Adorn It); mini page pebbles (Memories in the Making); die-cut tag (QuicKutz); rub-on flower (Maisy Mo); chalk ink (Clearsnap); glitter glue, liquid pearl (Ranger); floss (DMC); adhesive foam (Therm O Web); liquid adhesive (Magic Scraps)

JUST A NOTE 17
Supplies: Cardstock (Bazzill); ribbon (Chatterbox, Textured Trios); rickrack (Memories in the Making); die-cut photo corners (QuicKutz); ink (Clearsnap, Ranger); thread; adhesive foam (Therm O Web); liquid adhesive (Magic Scraps); Pharmacy font (Internet download)

TIA 18
Supplies: Patterned papers (Sweetwater); acrylic letters (Zsiage); chipboard hearts (Making Memories); word stamps (Heidi Swapp); letter stamps (PSX); date stamps (Just Rite); distress ink (Ranger); chalk ink (Clearsnap); walnut ink (7 Gypsies); ribbon (Creative Impressions); adhesive (Magic Scraps, Therm O Web); muslin; note paper; paper clips; 2Ps Cocoa, 2Ps GG's Love Me font (Two Peas in a Bucket); Garamond font (Microsoft)

JOY 18
Supplies: Album, hinge (7 Gypsies); cardstock; patterned papers (Melissa Francis); chipboard letters (Zsiage); die-cut letters (QuicKutz); paint (Li'l Davis); liquid pearl (Ranger); lace; ribbon (American Crafts); velvet trip (Creative Impressions); paper flowers (Serendipity Design Works); dye (Making Memories); adhesives (Magic Scraps, Therm O Web, Xyron)

FUN DAY 19
Supplies: Cardstock (Paper Adventures); patterned papers (Sandylion); chipboard letters (Heidi Swapp, Li'l Davis); rub-on letters (Imagination Project); clipboard (Provo Craft); chipboard photo corners (Junkitz); die-cut heart, index tab (QuicKutz); photo turns (7 Gypsies); cheese cloth (Wimpole Street Creations); rickrack (Creative Impressions); date stamp (Making Memories); dimensional glaze, distress ink (Ranger); brads (Bazzill); staples; twine (American Hemp); adhesives (Magic Scraps, Therm O Web); Teimpo font (Internet download)

THE BUTTERFLY FARM 20
Supplies: White cardstock, brads, monochromatic ink (Bazzill); all other papers (Scrapworks); chipboard letters (Li'l Davis); die-cut letters (QuicKutz); flourish stamp (Adorn It); stamping ink (Tsukineko); corner rounder; floss (DMC); adhesives (Magic Scraps, Therm O Web, Xyron); butterfly appliqués (unknown)

TIA – FAITHFUL FRIEND 22
Supplies: Chipboard book, wire flowers (Maya Road); chipboard letters (Making Memories, Zsiage); chipboard words (Li'l Davis); rub-on letters (Polar Bear Press); letter stamps (EK Success); date stamp (Just Rite); chipboard hearts (Heidi Swapp, Making Memories); die-cut flowers (QuicKutz); dog bone paper clips, photo turns, rickrack, velvet ribbon (Creative Impressions); twill (Scenic Route); ribbon (May Arts); floss (DMC); acrylic flowers, patterned brads (Queen & Co.); solid brads (Bazzill); sequin hearts (Doodlebug); pearl finish (DecoArt); dye, paint (Making Memories); chalk ink (Clearsnap); liquid glue (Magic Scraps); beads; cotton batting; fabric; four petal flowers (unknown); staples

FAMILY LOVE 23
Supplies: Cardstock, chipboard circle (Bazzill); chipboard letters (Everlasting Keepsakes); rub-on letters (Imagination Project); ribbon, rickrack (Maya Road); acrylic heart, photo corners (Heidi Swapp); chipboard heart, dye, paint (Making Memories); die-cut tag (QuicKutz); buttons (SEI); floss (DMC); chalk ink (Clearsnap); distress ink (Ranger); adhesives (Therm O Web); cotton batting; fabric; silk flower; 2Ps Beef Broccoli font (Two Peas in a Bucket)

THANK YOU 24
Supplies: Cardstock (Bazzill); silk flowers (Heidi Swapp); ribbon (May Arts); glitter glue (Ranger); letter stamps (Hero Arts); chalk ink (Clearsnap); adhesives (Magic Scraps, Therm O Web) crystals (unknown)

BROWN TAPESTRY 24
Supplies: Mini book (Bazzill); cardstock; flowers (Petaloo); bookplate, rub-on (BasicGrey); large brad (All My Memories); small brads (Creative Impressions); black trim (Venus Industries); die-cut tag (QuicKutz); glitter glue (Ranger); chalk ink (Clearsnap); jump ring, safety pin (Making Memories); adhesives (Therm O Web)

FUN LOVING YOUTH 25

Supplies: Cardstock (Bazzill); patterned paper (Daisy D's); transparency (Creative Imaginations); blue flower (Prima); cream flowers (Serendipity Design Works); rub-on flowers (Polar Bear Press); chipboard ampersand (Making Memories); ribbon (May Arts); twill (Scenic Route); rub-on flourish and words (BasicGrey); brads, photo turns (Creative Impressions); chipboard, flower, lace, metal washers, die-cut typewriter letter (unknown) chalk ink (Clearsnap); adhesives (Magic Scraps, Therm O Web)

TREASURE YOUR FAMILY 26

Supplies: Cardstock, chipboard tiles (Bazzill); patterned papers (We R Memory Keepers); letter stickers (Autumn Leaves); die-cut hearts and letters (QuicKutz); photo anchors (7 Gypsies); ribbon slide (Maya Road); rub-on phrase (Scenic Route); chalk ink (Clearsnap); brads (Creative Impressions); adhesives (Therm O Web); chipboard; fibers; P22 Typewriter font (Internet download)

HEIDI & TRUDY 27

Supplies: Patterned papers, letter stickers, monogram letters, ribbon (BasicGrey); fibers (Yarn Collection); flowers (Petaloo); index tab, photo anchors, rub-on post marks, spiral clips, wax seal (7 Gypsies); mini brads (Creative Impressions); jumbo brads (All My Memories); distress ink (Ranger); chalk ink (Clearsnap); liquid glue (Magic Scraps); adhesives (Therm O Web); Zapf Humanist BT font (Internet download)

CHAPTER 2 METALS

ELEPHANTS OF THE DESERT 30

Supplies: Cardstock; patterned paper, die-cut tag, ribbons (Fancy Pants); die-cut brackets, index tab, letters (QuicKutz); wire (Artistic Wire); wire elephant (Pier 1); date stamp (Just Rite); paper crimper (Fiskars); brads (Creative Impressions); charm, jump ring (unknown); chalk ink (Clearsnap); adhesive (Therm O Web); liquid adhesive (Magic Scraps); Caslon Antique font (Internet download)

ALEX & ARCHERY 31

Supplies: Cardstock (Bazzill); patterned papers, letter stickers (BasicGrey); chipboard letters (Li'l Davis); brads (Creative Impressions); photo anchors (7 Gypsies); die-cut tag accent (QuicKutz); twine (American Hemp); date stamp (Just Rite); distress ink (Ranger); chalk ink (Clearsnap); liquid glue (Magic Scraps); adhesive foam (Therm O Web); wire (unknown); Ransom Group Antique font (Internet download)

JUST HANGIN' OUT 32

Supplies: Cardstock; patterned papers (Adorn It); chipboard letters (Heidi Swapp, Scenic Route); die-cut flowers, letters, photo anchors, photo corners (QuicKutz); rub-on flowers (Maisy Mo); brads (Bazzill, Making Memories); chalk ink (Clearsnap); glass finish (Plaid); date stamp (Just Rite); adhesives (Therm O Web, Xyron); transparency; staples; Gandy Dancer font (Internet download)

MONSTER JUNGLE BUGGY 33

Supplies: Patterned paper (Sandylion); letter stamps (Gel-a-tins); die-cut letters, nameplate (QuicKutz); screw top brads (Karen Foster); rub-on letters (Imagination Project); photo anchors (7 Gypsies); ink (Ranger); twine (American Hemp); date stamp (Just Rite); adhesive foam (Therm O Web); mini brads (Creative Impressions); shipping tags, metal mesh, metal washers (unknown)

FOREVER FRIENDS 34

Supplies: Cardstock (Bazzill); letter stickers, patterned paper (Chatterbox); die-cut letters (QuicKutz); brads, flowers, paint (Making Memories); screw top brads (Karen Foster); pewter brads, photo anchors (Creative Impressions); rub-ons (7 Gypsies); corner brackets (Stanley); adhesives (Magic Scraps, Therm O Web, Xyron); lace; staples; washers

NOTES FROM ALEX 35

Supplies: CD tin (Scraptivity); patterned and solid papers (Keeping Memories Alive); chipboard letters (Pressed Petals); letter stamps (PSX); paint (Making Memories); die-cut letters, tag (QuicKutz); screw top brads (Karen Foster); rub-on stitching (7 Gypsies); chalk ink (Clearsnap); liquid adhesive (Magic Scraps); double sided tape (Therm O Web); computer font (Times New Roman); bracket, charm, hinge, jump ring, metallic rickrack (unknown); muslin; pen

technique tip 35

Supplies: Brackets (Stanley); paint (Li'l Davis); patterned papers (Chatterbox); alcohol inks, copper mixative, distress embossing ink, distress embossing powder (Ranger); rub-on numbers (My Minds Eye); nail heads (American Tag); screw top brads (Karen Foster); antique copper brads (Creative Imaginations); eyelets

SEAWORLD 36

Supplies: Cardstock, chipboard circles, brads (Bazzill); embossing metal sheet (K&S Engineering); alcohol inks, blending solution, pearl mixative (Ranger); chipboard letters (Zsiage); rub-on letters (Making Memories); mini page pebbles (Memories in the Making); photo anchors (7 Gypsies); liquid adhesive (Magic Scraps); Rataczak font (Internet download)

THANK YOU CARD 37

Supplies: Cardstock (Bazzill); metal sheet (K&S Engineering); die-cut tile, embossing die (QuicKutz); acrylic heart (Heidi Grace); dimensional glaze, distress ink (Ranger); chalk ink (Clearsnap); photo corners (3L); ribbon (May Arts); adhesive (Therm O Web)

HOME SWEET HOME 38

Supplies: Box book (Junkitz); patterned papers (Adorn It); door handle, "home" flashcard, key hole, photo anchor, walnut ink (7 Gypsies); die-cut flourishes, letters, photo corners, tab (QuicKutz); distress ink (Ranger); chalk ink (Clearsnap); brads, metal molding, paint (Making Memories); flowers (Serendipity Design Works); button, linen thread (Hillcreek); adhesives (Magic Scraps, Therm O Web, Xyron); muslin

TRUE LOVE 39

Supplies: Cardstock (Prism); patterned papers (Daisy D's); metal molding (Making Memories); tag (We R Memory Keepers); metallic paint (Li'l Davis); flowers (Petaloo); die-cut scrolls, stars (QuicKutz); brads, photo turns (Creative Impressions); metal embossing template (Ten Seconds Studio); glass finishing glaze (Plaid); embossing metal (K&S Engineering); distress ink (Ranger); walnut ink (7 Gypsies); ribbon (Michaels); adhesive foam (Therm O Web); liquid adhesive (Magic Scraps); lace (unknown)

TOGETHERNESS 40

Supplies: Cardstock (Bazzill); metal words (Making Memories); texture paste (Delta Creative); chipboard heart (Heidi Swapp); die-cut parentheses (QuicKutz); brads (Creative Impressions); chalk ink (Clearsnap); adhesive (Therm O Web); liquid adhesive (Magic Scraps); chipboard; staples; thread; Times New Roman font (Microsoft)

ALEX 41

Supplies: Patterned papers (BasicGrey); large metal letters, vellum (Bazzill); small metal letters, paint, square brads (Making Memories); charms; wavy ruler (Plaid); chalk ink (Clearsnap); buttons (7 Gypsies); floss (DMC); dimensional glaze (Ranger); date stamp (Just Rite); vellum adhesive (Therm O Web); liquid adhesive (Magic Scraps); Smite font (Internet download)

GRAND CAYMAN 42

Supplies: Patterned paper (Me & My Big Ideas); monogram "C", paint, stick pins (Making Memories); chipboard letters (Making Memories, Zsiage); distress embossing ink, distress embossing powder, Van Dyke brown ink (Ranger); coastal netting, liquid adhesive (Magic Scraps); cheesecloth (Wimpole Street Creations); brads, twill tape (Creative Impressions); twine (American Hemp); adhesive foam (Therm O Web); Rataczak Condensed font (Internet download)

technique tip 43

Supplies: Charms (Magenta); metallic leafing pens (Krylon)

MY SWEET GIRL 43

Supplies: Cardstock, chipboard circle (Bazzill); patterned papers, diecuts (Sassafras Lass); metal border strip (Provo Craft); die-cut letters, photo anchors, photo corners, tab, tag accents (QuicKutz); ribbon (American Crafts); rickrack (Memories in the Making); flower (Heidi Swapp); brads, dog bone paper clip (Creative Impressions); rub-ons (BasicGrey); glitter glue (Ranger); chalk ink (Clearsnap); adhesives (Therm O Web, Xyron); hole punch (We R Memory Keepers); charms; jump rings; safety pin; staples; Scrap Simple font (Internet download)

THE WHITE TIGERS OF LAS VEGAS 44

Supplies: Cardstock (Bazzill); patterned papers (Polar Bear Press); chipboard flourishes (Everlasting Keepsakes); paint (Li'l Davis); book clip, ribbon (BasicGrey); die-cut letters (QuicKutz); brads, photo anchors (Creative Impressions); distress ink (Ranger); adhesives (Therm O Web, Xyron); Alter Regular font (Internet download)

AYSHA 44
Supplies: Cardstock, chipboard rectangle (Bazzill); ribbon (Michaels); chipboard flower (Everlasting Keepsakes); paint (Li'l Davis); metal molding strip (Provo Craft); die-cut letters (QuicKutz); brads (Making Memories); eyelets, jewels (unknown); nail head (American Tag); dimensional glaze, distress ink (Ranger); adhesive foam (Therm O Web); hole punch (We R Memory Keepers); liquid adhesive (Magic Scraps)

PRINCESS CHLOE 45
Supplies: Cardstock, brads, button, chipboard circle (Bazzill); Patterned paper, index tab template (Provo Craft); ribbon (May Arts); plastic letters (Heidi Swapp); die-cut photo corners, photo anchors (QuicKutz); sequin hearts, small eyelets (Doodlebug); silver eyelets (Creative Imaginations); decorative scissors (Fiskars); distress ink (Ranger); Angelina fibers (Meadowbrook Inventions); adhesives (Magic Scraps, Therm O Web); Auburn font (Internet download)

CHAPTER 3 NATURAL ELEMENTS

WISHING YOU... 48
Supplies: Papers (Polar Bear Press); flowers (Nature's Pressed); mica (USArtQuest); twine (American Hemp); distress ink (Ranger); brads (ScrapArts); adhesive foam (Therm O Web); liquid adhesive (Magic Scraps); AllisonROB font (Internet download)

A LITTLE BIRDIE TOLD ME 48
Supplies: Patterned and pink cardstock (Polar Bear Press); white cardstock (Bazzill); dried flower (Nature's Pressed); microscope slides (Memories in the Making); ribbon (All My Memories); chalk ink (Clearsnap); copper leafing pen (Krylon); metallic leafing flakes (Biblical Impressions); floss (DMC); adhesive tape, adhesive dots (Therm O Web); liquid adhesive (Magic Scraps); Verdana font (Microsoft)

SISTERS 49
Supplies: Cardstock (Bazzill); dried flowers (Nature's Pressed); cheesecloth (Wimpole Street Creations); Adirondack wash, dye ink (Ranger); twill tape (Scenic Route); vellum tags (Making Memories); heart ribbon slide (Maya Road); photo turns (7 Gypsies); brads (Creative Impressions); chalk ink (Clearsnap); dimensional foam tape, adhesive dots (Therm O Web); adhesives (Magic Scraps, Xyron); hole punch (We R Memory Keepers); metal mesh; staples; AlexBrush, Inkster fonts (Internet download)

INUKSHUKS OF SALT SPRING ISLAND 50
Supplies: Cardstock (Bazzill); patterned papers (Junkitz); mica tiles (USArtQuest); letter stamps (Gel-a-tins); date stamp, eyelets (Making Memories); die-cut index tab (QuicKutz); epoxy letter sticker, paperclip (Li'l Davis); twine (American Hemp); brads (Creative Impressions); chalk ink (Clearsnap); distress ink (Ranger); solvent ink (Tsukineko); liquid adhesive (Magic Scraps); hole punch/setting tool (We R Memory Keepers); circle punch (EK Success); AL Worn Machine font (Internet download)

FIRE 51
Supplies: Cardstock (Bazzill); mica tiles (USArtQuest); border stickers, patterned paper (Sandylion); transparency (Grafix); chipboard letters (Heidi Swapp); rub-on letters (Imagination Project); metallic paint (Li'l Davis); die-cut index tab (QuicKutz); brads (Creative Impressions); photo anchors (7 Gypsies); date stamp (Just Rite); ink (Tsukineko); liquid adhesive (Magic Scraps); hole punch tool (We R Memory Keepers); Mayflower font (Internet download)

GATOR-LAND 52
Supplies: Cardstock; patterned paper (BasicGrey); burlap (Panacea); chipboard letters (Heidi Swapp); die-cut letters (QuicKutz); die-cut index tab (Provo Craft); photo turns (Creative Impressions); brads (Bazzill); muslin; walnut ink (7 Gypsies); distress ink (Ranger); adhesive (Therm O Web); liquid adhesive (Magic Scraps); P22 Typewriter font (Internet download)

SATURNA ISLAND 53
Supplies: Cardstock; patterned papers (We R Memory Keepers); mask (Heidi Swapp); jump ring, paint, safety pin (Making Memories); twill letters and tape (Adorn It); photo turns, walnut ink (7 Gypsies); twine (American Hemp); brads (Creative Impressions); distress ink (Ranger); charm (unknown); Chelt Press font (Internet download)

technique tip 53
Supplies: Patterned paper (Imagination Project); border stamp (Fontwerks); chipboard heart, eyelets (Making Memories); ribbon (May Arts); solvent ink (Tsukineko); distress ink, dimensional glaze (Ranger); dried flowers (Nature's Pressed); rub-on image (Polar Bear Press); chipboard frame (Maya Road); rub-on quote (Scenic Route); mask (Heidi Swapp); Instant Age Varnish (Delta Creative); adhesive (Magic Scraps)

ESCAPE 54
Supplies: Frame (Melissa Frances); fish netting, large shells, starfish (U.S. Shell); small shells, liquid adhesive (Magic Scraps); chipboard letters (Zsiage); cork (Creative Impressions); burning tool (Walnut Hollow); adhesive tape (Therm O Web); fabric, stones (unknown)

AT THE PATCH 55
Supplies: Cardstock (Bazzill); cork, brads, tape measure twill tape (Creative Impressions); chipboard letters (Autumn Leaves); die-cut letters (QuicKutz); photo turns, rub-ons, walnut ink (7 Gypsies); ribbon (SEI); fiber (Rubba Dub Dub); burning tool (Walnut Hollow); distress ink (Ranger); date stamp (Just Rite); muslin, shipping tags, twine (unknown); liquid adhesive (Magic Scraps); adhesive foam (Therm O Web); P22 Typewriter font (Internet download)

COASTAL LIVING 56
Supplies: Patterned paper (Sandylion); letter stickers, burlap ribbon (Me & My Big Ideas); brads, eyelets, photo turns (Making Memories); die-cut letters (QuicKutz); twine (American Hemp); date stamp (Just Rite); distress ink (Ranger); shell, liquid adhesive (Magic Scraps); other adhesives (Therm O Web, Xyron); hole punch, eyelet setting tool (We R Memory Keepers); twill tape; metal mesh; wood sheet; Sharpie font (Internet download)

THE STORY OF MY FAMILY 57
Supplies: Album, tag (7 Gypsies); patterned paper (Crate Paper); wooden flower (Provo Craft); fabric strips (Maisy Mo); walnut ink dauber (Fiber Scraps); large brad (All My Memories); chipboard heart, eyelets (Making Memories); paper flowers (Serendipity Design Works); cheesecloth (Wimpole Street Creations); die-cut photo turns (QuicKutz); rub-ons (Autumn Leaves); twine (American Hemp); distress ink (Ranger); ribbon (Creative Impressions, May Arts, Maya Road, My Mind's Eye, Textured Trios); twill (Adorn It); rickrack (Creative Impressions); liquid adhesive (Magic Scraps); mini brads; lace; wood sheet

DISNEY'S WILD LIFE 57
Supplies: Cardstock; Wood mesh (Natures Greetings); cork, brads (Creative Impressions); letter stamps (Ma Vinci's Reliquary); chipboard letters (Li'l Davis); die-cut letters (QuicKutz); paint (Making Memories); date stamp (Just Rite); ribbon (Textured Trios); distress ink (Ranger); walnut ink crystals (7 Gypsies); photo turns (Scrappin' Extras); adhesive foam and tape (Therm O Web); liquid adhesive (Magic Scraps); handmade paper; snap tape; P22 Typewriter font (Internet download)

CATCHING CRABS 58
Supplies: Cardstock; patterned paper (Me & My Big Ideas); fish netting (U.S. Shell); sponge stamps (Li'l Davis); paint, safety pin, eyelets (Making Memories); distress ink, dimensional glaze (Ranger); ink (Tsukineko); sandpaper (Norton); date stamp (Just Rite); twine (American Hemp); linen thread (Hillcreek); hole punch/eyelet setter (We R Memory Keepers); adhesive (Magic Scraps, Therm O Web); metal beads; SandraOh font (Internet download)

MY WISH FOR YOU 60
Supplies: Patterned papers, die-cut strips (Crate Paper); chipboard letters (Zsiage); die-cut letters, tab (QuicKutz); chipboard flowers (Everlasting Keepsakes); pearl brads (SEI); mini brads, photo turns (Creative Impressions); hemp twine (American Hemp); circle punches (EK Success); date stamp (Making Memories); distress ink (Ranger); chalk ink (Clearsnap); liquid adhesive (Magic Scraps); other adhesives (Therm O Web, Xyron); OohBaby font (Internet download)

LOVE 61
Supplies: Paper bag (DMD); border stamps (Tin Box Creations); "love" stamp (Gel-a-tins); twill tape (Maya Road); die-cut heart and jewelry tag (QuicKutz); chalk (Pebbles); distress ink (Ranger); solvent ink (Tsukineko); stick pins (Making Memories); linen thread (Hillcreek); hemp twine (American Hemp); eyelet, shipping tag (unknown); die-cut tag reinforcement (Accu-Cut); adhesive (Magic Scraps)

THE ALASKAN OUTHOUSE 61
Supplies: Cardstock (Bazzill); patterned papers (Adorn It, Déjà Views, We R Memory Keepers); chipboard letters (Everlasting Keepsakes); twill tape (Adorn It, Maya Road); burlap (Panacea); hemp twine (American Hemp); brads, paper clip (Creative Impressions); date stamp (Just Rite); distress ink (Ranger); chalk ink (Clearsnap); dimensional glaze (Plaid); adhesives (Magic Scraps, Therm O Web); beads; eyelets; Attic font (Internet download)

JUST RELAX 62
Supplies: Cardstock, mini brads (Bazzill); patterned paper (Li'l Davis); mesh (Magenta); letter stamps (PSX); date stamp (Just Rite); rub-on letters (My Minds Eye, Polar Bear Press); photo turns, profile card, walnut ink crystals (7 Gypsies); muslin flower (Junkitz); black ribbon (Me & My Big Ideas); stripe ribbon (May Arts); chalk ink (Clearsnap); distress ink (Ranger); solvent ink (Tsukineko); twine (American Hemp); linen thread (Hillcreek); adhesive dots (Therm O Web); liquid adhesive (Magic Scraps); buckle, buttons, charm, eyelet, lace (unknown); jump ring; muslin

ROAD TRIP 63
Supplies: Cardstock, chipboard circle (Bazzill); patterned paper, letter stickers (Memories Complete); mesh (Magenta); chalk ink (Clearsnap); distress ink, raspberry liquid pearl (Ranger); ribbon (Maya Road); die-cut brackets, paper clip and photo turns (QuicKutz); adhesive foam (Therm O Web); liquid adhesive (Magic Scraps); brads, eyelets, floral trim (unknown); transparency; Rataczak font (Internet download)

CHAPTER 4 ART MEDIUMS

BOSTON MARKET 66
Supplies: Patterned papers (Sandylion); antiquing gel, crackle finish, liquid adhesive (Delta Creative); transparency (Grafix); chipboard letters, date stamp, eyelets, paint (Making Memories); epoxy letters (Li'l Davis); dimensional glaze (Plaid); coastal netting (Magic Scraps); die-cut index tab (Provo Craft); hemp twine (American Hemp); twine ribbon (Me & My Big Ideas); distress ink (Ranger); brads (Creative Impressions); circle punch; photo turns (7 Gypsies); vellum adhesive (Therm O Web); metal washers; SandraOh font (Internet download)

AYSHA AT ELK LAKE 67
Supplies: Cardstock (Bazzill); crackle medium, liquid adhesive (Delta Creative); rub-on letters (American Crafts); rub-on words (Scenic Route); brads, safety pin, white paint (Making Memories); chipboard flourishes (Fancy Pants); pewter paint (Li'l Davis); flower (Heidi Swapp); rub-on flourishes (BasicGrey); Adirondack wash, distress ink (Ranger); index tab, photo turns (7 Gypsies); ribbon; wire mesh; National Archive font (Internet download)

CARVING 68
Supplies: Cardstock, chipboard tiles (Bazzill); texture paste (Delta Creative); mica flakes (Arnold Grummer's); chipboard letters (Li'l Davis); mini letters (Heidi Swapp); brads (Creative Impressions); photo turns (7 Gypsies); chalk ink (Clearsnap); adhesive (Therm O Web); pallet knife (DecoArt)

LOVE 69
Supplies: Cardstock, chipboard square (Bazzill); antiquing gel, texture paste (Delta Creative); patterned papers, stickers (Sandylion); lace (unknown); distress ink (Ranger); foam stamp (Making Memories); brads, photo turns (Creative Impressions); walnut ink crystals (7 Gypsies); transparency (Grafix); adhesive foam (Therm O Web); liquid adhesive (Delta Creative)

technique tip 69
Supplies: Patterned paper (Sassafras Lass); texture paste (Delta Creative); brad, cardstock, chipboard tiles (Bazzill); rub-ons (Maisy Mo); snowflake mask (Heidi Swapp); die-cut heart (QuicKutz); chipboard letter (Zsiage); chipboard circle (Maya Road); dimensional glaze, glitter glue, pink pearl (Ranger); adhesive foam (Therm O Web)

2008 DAY PLANNER 70
Supplies: Chipboard album (Maya Road); patterned papers, number stickers (All My Memories); die-cut letters (QuicKutz); Makin's Clay (Sino Harvest); texture template (Adorn It); distress ink, dimensional glaze (Ranger); paint (Making Memories); brads (Creative Impressions); metal index tabs, walnut ink crystals (7 Gypsies); adhesive (Therm O Web); corner rounder (McGill); lace; ribbon

ON ANY GIVEN SUNDAY 71
Supplies: Patterned papers, rickrack, twill (Provo Craft); Makin's Clay (Sino Harvest); circle and flower cutters, finishing glaze (DecoArt); texture template (Adorn It); chipboard letters (Zsiage); distress ink, glitter glue, liquid pearl (Ranger); ribbon (May Arts); rub-on hearts (Polar Bear Press); paint (Plaid); floss (DMC); brads (Bazzill, Making Memories); die-cut photo turns (QuicKutz); adhesive (Magic Scraps, Therm O Web); Scrap Simple font (Internet download)

HOME 72
Supplies: Cardstock; patterned paper, transparency (K&Co.); transfer ink (Stewart Superior); chipboard letters (Heidi Swapp, Li'l Davis); paint (Making Memories); brads, photo turns (Creative Impressions); chalk ink (Clearsnap); distress ink (Ranger); dimensional glaze (Plaid); rub-ons (BasicGrey); adhesives (Therm O Web); Cheryl font (Internet download)

FAVORITE PHOTOS 74
Supplies: Cardstock (Bazzill); patterned papers (Polar Bear Press); fibers, glitters, Paper Perfect (DecoArt); letter stickers (American Crafts); die-cut letters, photo corners (QuicKutz); fabric strip (Maisy Mo); buckle (Sunshine Designs); chipboard flowers (Li'l Davis); eyelet, paper lace (unknown); chalk ink (Clearsnap); snaps (Chatterbox); adhesives (Magic Scraps, Therm O Web, Xyron)

FRIENDSHIP CARD 75
Supplies: Cardstock (Bazzill); fibers, glitters, Paper Perfect (DecoArt); chipboard mold, rickrack (Maya Road); chipboard flowers (Li'l Davis); fabric label (Me & My Big Ideas); Adirondack wash (Ranger); brad (Creative Impressions); chalk ink (Clearsnap); staples; adhesives (Therm O Web)

THE BIRDS OF CRYSTAL GARDENS 76
Supplies: Cardstock, chipboard circle (Bazzill); die-cut circle, patterned papers, ribbon (Fancy Pants); alcohol inks, applicator tool, blending solution, dimensional glaze, distress ink (Ranger); letter stickers (American Crafts); rub-on letters (Imagination Project); die-cut index tab (QuicKutz); brads, photo turns (Creative Impressions); date stamp (Just Rite); acid free document mending tape (3M); adhesive glue lines (Therm O Web)

BRR... 77
Supplies: Patterned papers (Sandylion); letters (Zsiage); alcohol inks, applicator tool, blending solution, dimensional glaze, glitter glue (Ranger); acrylic snowflakes (Heidi Swapp); acrylic photo turns (Junkitz); transparency (Grafix); paper tearing ruler (Plaid); vellum adhesive (Therm O Web); Times New Roman font (Microsoft)

COSTA MAYA 78
Supplies: Cardstock (Bazzill); metallic leafing flakes (Biblical Impressions); chipboard brackets (BasicGrey); die-cut letters (QuicKutz); buttons; distress ink (Ranger); dimensional glaze (Plaid); paint (Making Memories); spray adhesive (Krylon); dimensional foam (Therm O Web)

TREASURE 79
Supplies: Frame (PageFrame); cardstock (Bazzill); patterned papers (We R Memory Keepers); metallic leafing flakes (Biblical Impressions); brads, chipboard letters, heart, mask (Heidi Swapp); eyelets (unknown); dimensional glaze, glitter glue (Ranger); ribbon (May Arts); ink (Clearsnap, Tsukineko); buckle (Sunshine Designs); spray adhesive (Krylon); adhesive dots, dimensional foam (Therm O Web)

SHOPPING, MEXICAN STYLE 80
Supplies: Cardstock (Bazzill); muslin; batik resist medium (Crafter's Pick); die-cut flower (Deluxe Designs); Adirondack wash, dimensional glaze, distress ink (Ranger); foam stamps (Junkitz, Making Memories); faux leather strip (Li'l Davis); twill (Scenic Route); letter stamps (Gel-a-tins); rub-on letters (Adorn It); page pebbles (Memories in the Making); date stamp (Making Memories); transparency (Grafix); brads (Creative Impressions); staples

ERIKIA 82
Supplies: Patterned papers (BasicGrey); chipboard letters (Zsiage); battenburg lace (SEI); color wash, clear dimensional glaze (Ranger); lilac dimensional glaze (Plaid); chipboard photo corners (Junkitz); brad, velvet ribbon (Creative Impressions); chalk ink (Clearsnap); adhesives (Magic Scraps, Therm O Web); white lace; 2Ps Quick font (Internet download)

FRIENDS TIN 83
Supplies: Lunch box (Maya Road); flourish and letter stickers, metal washer, metal chain, patterned papers (Making Memories); glitter glue, clear dimensional glaze, Adirondack wash (Ranger); rhinestone brad (SEI); rhinestones, silk flowers (unknown); chalk ink (Clearsnap); adhesives (Magic Scraps, Therm O Web); ribbons (May Arts, Michaels); metal zipper pull (All My Memories); muslin strips; corner rounder

BLUE CARD 83
Supplies: Cardstock (Bazzill); cotton square; Adirondack wash, glitter glue (Ranger); rub-ons (Chatterbox); rhinestone brad (SEI); chalk ink (Clearsnap); adhesives (Therm O Web)

CHAPTER 5 PAPER

FATHER FROST 86
Supplies: Cardstock, brads (Bazzill); patterned papers (Chatterbox); letter stickers (American Crafts); acrylic snowflakes (Heidi Grace); photo turns (Creative Impressions); chalk ink (Clearsnap); die-cut photo corners (QuicKutz); glitter glue (Ranger); dimensional glaze (Plaid); adhesives (Therm O Web); American Writer font (Internet download)

technique tip 86
Supplies: Cardstock (Bazzill); patterned papers (Junkitz); die-cut letters (QuicKutz); wire (Artistic Wire); dimensional glaze, glitter glue (Ranger); decorative scissors (Fiskars); pen (Sakura); adhesives (Therm O Web, Xyron); Arrow dingbat, Silly Fill In, You Are Here fonts (Internet download)

HAPPY BIRTHDAY CARD 87
Supplies: Cardstock, brads, chipboard circle (Bazzill); cardstock stickers, patterned papers (Sandylion); cutting template (Lacé); chalk ink (Clearsnap); glitter glue (Ranger); adhesives (Therm O Web)

ALL ABOUT ME ALBUM 87
Supplies: D-Ring album (American Crafts); cardstock, mini brads (Bazzill); fabric strips, patterned papers, photo corners (Imagination Project); chipboard letters (Zsiage); die-cut letters (QuicKutz); large brads (Creative Impressions); chalk ink (Clearsnap); dimensional glaze (Plaid); glitter glue (Ranger); adhesives (Krylon, Magic Scraps, Therm O Web, Xyron)

FREEZE TIME 88
Supplies: Patterned papers (Melissa Frances); chipboard letters (Heidi Swapp, unknown); epoxy letter sticker (Li'l Davis); chipboard corners, flat pin, measuring tape, muslin flower (Junkitz); clear buttons, date sticker, parenthesis card, photo turns, rub-ons (7 Gypsies); paint (Making Memories); letter stamps (PSX); rolling letter stamps (Provo Craft); date stamp (Just Rite); distress ink (Ranger); stamping ink (Tsukineko); brads, ribbon (Creative Impressions); handmade paper; heart; lace; manila tag

THANKFUL 89
Supplies: Cardstock (Bazzill); patterned paper (Making Memories); chipboard photo corners (Junkitz); rub-on flourishes (BasicGrey); ribbon (May Arts); die-cut photo turns (QuicKutz); chalk ink (Clear Snap); brads (Creative Impressions); adhesive (Therm O Web); jewels, specialty papers (unknown); Prissy Frat Boy font (Internet download); Times New Roman font (Microsoft)

RACHEL 90
Lyrics by: Leann Womack
Supplies: Cardstock, brads (Bazzill); watercolor paper (Strathmore); chipboard letters, flowers (Melissa Frances); Adirondack wash (Ranger); die-cut letters, index tab (QuicKutz); chipboard brackets (Fancy Pants); faux leather strip (Li'l Davis); ink (Clearsnap); photo turns (7 Gypsies); epoxy charm (Making Memories); date stamp (Just Rite); dimensional glaze (Plaid); adhesive foam (Therm O Web); adhesives (Magic Scraps, Xyron)

PARIS 92
Supplies: Cardstock, black brads (Bazzill); metal letters (American Crafts); chipboard flourish (Fancy Pants); photo corner (Scrapworks); ribbon, ribbon buckle (Maya Road); sliver brads, photo turns (Creative Impressions); ink (Clearsnap); dimensional glaze (Ranger); hole punches (Making Memories); adhesive (Therm O Web)

THINK PINK 93
Supplies: Cardstock (Bazzill, Doodlebug); epoxy stickers, patterned papers, twill trimmings (Provo Craft); chipboard letters (Heidi Swapp); letter stamps (Gel-a-tins); paint, hole punches (Making Memories); chipboard flourishes (Fancy Pants); dimensional glaze (Plaid); glitter glue (Ranger); adhesive foam, other adhesives (Therm O Web);

OUR FAMILY TIES 94
Supplies: Cardstock, patterned papers (Crate Paper); chipboard letters (Zsiage); die-cut letters (QuicKutz); chipboard stars (Heidi Swapp); gold dimensional paint (DecoArt); photo turns (7 Gypsies); ribbon (May Arts); distress ink (Ranger); brads (Bazzill); adhesives (Therm O Web, Xyron); Textbook font (Internet download)

CANADA'S ICE QUEEN 95
Supplies: White core paper (Collage Press); cardstock (Bazzill); flowers, acrylic letters (Heidi Swapp); alcohol inks, blending solution, glitter glue (Ranger); embossing die (QuicKutz); photo turns (7 Gypsies); brads (Bazzill, Creative Impressions); Bembo font (Internet download)

4 PAWS 96
Supplies: Chipboard album, "4", flower jewel, strips (Heidi Swapp); chipboard letters (Scenic Route); paint (Plaid); satin varnish (DecoArt); die-cut heart (QuicKutz); rub-on letters (Adorn It); dimensional glaze, glitter glue (Ranger); ribbon (American Crafts, May Arts, Maya Road); adhesives (Magic Scraps, Therm O Web); flower (unknown)

JELLY FISH 97
Supplies: Cardstock (Bazzill); large chipboard letters (Zsiage); small chipboard letters (Heidi Swapp); rub-on letters (Scenic Route); circle stamps (Adorn It, Tin Box Creations); blue dimensional glaze (Plaid); clear dimensional glaze, glitter glue (Ranger); blue ink (Clearsnap); stamping ink (Tsukineko); adhesive (Magic Scraps)

PURE JOY 98
Supplies: Cardstock, brads (Bazzill); chipboard letters, patterned papers (Chatterbox); die-cut hearts, letters and photo turns, (QuicKutz); distress ink (Ranger); adhesive foam, double sided tape (Therm O Web); other adhesive (Xyron); cardboard; Angleterre Book font (Internet download)

technique tip 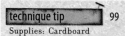 99
Supplies: Cardboard

THE HIGHLIGHT OF OUR TRIP 99
Supplies: Frame, title embellishment (Me & My Big Ideas); cardstock; cardboard; twine (American Hemp); brads, dog bone paper clip (Creative Impressions); distress ink (Ranger); adhesive foam (Therm O Web); P22 Typewriter font (Internet download)

MERRY CHRISTMAS 99
Supplies: Cardstock (Bazzill); acrylic star (Heidi Swapp); "Christmas" embellishment, rhinestones (Me & My Big Ideas); rub-on letters (Imagination Project); ribbon (American Crafts); chalk ink (Clearsnap); paint (Making Memories); dimensional glaze (Plaid); adhesive tape, adhesive foam (Therm O Web); cardboard; micro beads

SOUTH BEACH 100
Supplies: Cardstock, brads, chipboard circle (Bazzill); patterned paper (Paper Salon); white puffy paper (STYROFOAM® Brand Puffy Paper™ Thin Foam); texture template (Adorn It); letter stickers, rub-ons (Chatterbox); die-cut index tab (Provo Craft); die-cut letters, photo anchors (QuicKutz); dimensional glaze (Plaid); glitter glue (Ranger); buttons (7 Gypsies); page pebbles (Memories in the Making); adhesives (Magic Scraps, Xyron); 2Ps Flower Garden, Tiempo fonts (Internet download)

JUST CHILLIN' 101
Supplies: Cardstock; patterned papers (Sandylion); black puffy paper (STYROFOAM® Brand Puffy Paper™ Thin Foam); texture template (Adorn It); chipboard bracket (Making Memories); silver paint (Delta Creative); dimensional glaze (Plaid); letter stickers, rub-on letters (American Crafts); chalk ink (Clearsnap); solvent ink (Tsukineko); brads (Heidi Swapp); adhesive foam, double sided tape (Therm O Web); Palatino font (Internet download)

MAGIC 102
Supplies: Clipboard frame, date sticker, flash card, walnut ink crystals (7 Gypsies); cardstock; patterned paper (Cosmo Cricket); chipboard flourishes (Everlasting Keepsakes); muslin flower (Junkitz); rub-on flourish (Heidi Swapp); chipboard brackets (Me & My Big Ideas); walnut ink dauber (Fiber Scraps); distress ink (Ranger); chalk ink (Clearsnap); heart stamp (PSX); date stamp (Just Rite); adhesive (Therm O Web); distress tool (Making Memories); buttons; jewelry tag; muslin; P22 Typewriter font (Internet download)

technique tip 102

Supplies: Shipping tags; letter stamps (PSX); walnut ink crystals (7 Gypsies); stamping ink (Ranger); drink crystals (Kool-Aid); plastic wrap; salt

REAL LIFE GYPSIES 103

Supplies: Cardstock (Bazzill); distress ink (Ranger); chalk ink (Clearsnap); walnut ink crystals, photo anchors, wax seal (7 Gypsies); chipboard letters (Li'l Davis); chipboard flourish (Everlasting Keepsakes); battenburg lace (SEI); measuring tape twill, chipboard photo corners (Junkitz); distressed rub-on border (My Mind's Eye); paint, safety pin, eyelet, distress tool (Making Memories); date stamp (Just Rite); ribbon (Textured Trios); twine (American Hemp); shipping tags; brads (Creative Impressions); adhesive (Magic Scraps, Therm O Web); fine art matte photo paper (Ilford); P22 Typewriter font (Internet download)

CHAPTER 6 CLEAR ELEMENTS

KAREN 106

Supplies: Cardstock (Bazzill); patterned papers, chipboard stickers (Me & My Big Ideas); chipboard letters (Li'l Davis); brackets, die-cut letters, index tab, photo corners, (QuicKutz); liquid beads (DecoArt); ink (Clearsnap); dimensional glaze (Ranger); photo turns (7 Gypsies); brads (Creative Impressions); adhesives (Therm O Web, Xyron)

technique tip 107

Supplies: Cardstock (Bazzill); micro beads (Ranger); die-cut letters (QuicKutz); metal charm (Provo Craft); square punch (Creative Memories); rub-on letter (Scenic Route); chalk ink (Clear Snap); dimensional glaze (Plaid); wire (Artistic Wire); chipboard flower (Maya Road); ribbon (May Arts); Crop-a-dile hole punch (We R Memory Keepers); floss (DMC); adhesive sheet (Therm O Web); beads

LOVE THIS FAMILY 108

Supplies: Cardstock (Bazzill); chipboard letters (Everlasting Keepsakes); die-cut letters (QuicKutz); dimensional glaze, dimensional glitter paint (Plaid); heart sequins (Doodlebug); round sequins (Jewel Craft); heart charm (Heidi Grace); distress ink (Ranger); transparency (Grafix); adhesive (Magic Scraps, Xyron)

SMILE 109

Supplies: Patterned paper (Sassafras Lass); chipboard letters (Maya Road); brads, sequin flowers (Queen & Co.); die-cut letters (QuicKutz); rub-on letters (Adorn It); distress ink, glitter glue, liquid pearl (Ranger); dimensional glaze, paint (Plaid); rub-on arrow (Maisy Mo); photo turns (7 Gypsies); adhesive (Magic Scraps, Therm O Web, Xyron)

WARM WINTER WISHES 110

Supplies: Cardstock (Bazzill); patterned paper (Sassafras Lass); die-cut letters, embossing die, penguin and heart (QuicKutz); rickrack, brads (Creative Impressions); transparency (Grafix); dimensional glaze (Plaid); chalk ink (Clearsnap); adhesive (Therm O Web)

ALWAYS BELIEVE 110

Supplies: Cardstock (Bazzill); patterned paper (Scenic Route); letter stickers (American Crafts); rhinestone letters (Me & My Big Ideas); transparency (Grafix); chipboard hearts (Heidi Swapp); felt ribbon (Provo Craft); rub-on frame (Maisy Mo); die-cut photo anchors (QuicKutz); ink (Tsukineko); brads (Creative Impressions); paper crimper (Fiskars); adhesive (Therm O Web); FastPardon font (Internet download)

MEETING BRIAN 111

Supplies: Cardstock (Bazzill); index tab, patterned and solid papers, ribbon (SEI); transparency (Grafix); chipboard letters (Heidi Swapp); die-cut letters, photo corners, photo turns (QuicKutz); epoxy letter stickers, paper clips (Li'l Davis); distress ink, dimensional glaze (Ranger); letter stamps (PSX); date stamp (Just Rite); brads (Creative Impressions); adhesive (Therm O Web); AlterRegular font (Internet download)

EVERYDAY LIFE 112

Supplies: Landscape album (American Crafts); acrylic frame, acrylic letters, flowers, fuzzy rub-ons (Heidi Swapp); die-cut letters, index tab (QuicKutz); brads (Bazzill); rub-on dots (Maisy Mo); glitter glue (Ranger); letter stamps (PSX); chalk ink (Clearsnap); adhesive (Therm O Web, Xyron); ribbon

FAMILY 113

Supplies: Frame (Bazzill); acrylic charms (Heidi Grace); acrylic letters (Go West Studios); ribbon (American Crafts); rickrack (Creative Impressions); chalk ink (Clearsnap); glue lines (Therm O Web); liquid adhesive (Magic Scraps)

SITTING PRETTY 113

Supplies: Cardstock (Bazzill); patterned papers, rub-on shapes (Adorn It); acrylic flowers, acrylic letters, chipboard scroll, stripe ribbon (Maya Road); chipboard letters, photo corners, slide clips (Heidi Swapp); border stamp (Tin Box Creations); die-cut heart, embossing die, index tab (QuicKutz); Paper Effects paint (DecoArt); dimensional glaze, paint (Plaid); pearl brads (SEI); glitter rub-ons (Li'l Davis); ink (Tsukineko); pen (Sakura); dot ribbon (May Arts); silver mini brads (Creative Impressions); adhesive (Magic Scraps, Therm O Web); 2Ps Notebook font (Internet download)

GOTTA LOVE GRANDPA 114

Supplies: Patterned papers, brads, letter stickers, ribbon (All My Memories); die-cut letters, index tab (QuicKutz); distress ink (Ranger); solvent ink (Tsukineko); shrink plastic (Rose Art); brackets stamps (Tin Box Creations); date stamp (Just Rite); adhesive (Therm O Web, Xyron); Palatino font (Internet download)

technique tip 114

Supplies: Shrink plastic (Rose Art); opaque paint markers (Sakura); chipboard flower and heart shapes (Maya Road); rub-on letters and flowers (Imagination Project); rub-on dot border (Polar Bear Press); rhinestone brad (SEI); ribbon, silk flower (unknown); argyle border stamp (Sassafras Lass); flower stamp (Adorn It); glitter glue, liquid pearl (Ranger); solvent ink (Tsukineko); wire (Artistic Wire); rhinestones (Me & My Big Ideas); micro beads (DecoArt); decorative scissors (Fiskars); hole punch (We R Memory Keepers); 2Ps Doodads, 2Ps Halloween, Ding Bat fonts (Internet download)

THANK YOU! CARD 115

Supplies: Cardstock (Bazzill); shrink plastic (Rose Art); die-cut letters (QuicKutz); pens (Sakura); transparency (Grafix); distress ink, glitter glue (Ranger); adhesive (Therm O Web); 2Ps All Boxed Up, Ding Bat fonts (Internet download)

STAR DREAMER 115

Supplies: Cardstock (Bazzill); patterned papers (Sandylion); rub-on stars (Maisy Mo); letter stickers (Junkitz); shrink plastic (Rose Art); chipboard stars (Heidi Swapp); die-cut photo turns (QuicKutz); brads (Creative Impressions); distress ink, glitter glue (Ranger); adhesive (Therm O Web); 2Ps Ring Around, SP Sunday morning fonts (Internet download)

SNOW DAY 116

Supplies: Cardstock (Bazzill); patterned papers, chipboard letters (Scenic Route); glass slide mounts (Memories in the Making); alcohol inks, blending solution, glitter glue (Ranger); acrylic snowflakes, snowflake mask (Heidi Swapp); brads, photo turns (Creative Impressions); chalk ink (Clearsnap); adhesive (Magic Scraps, Therm O Web)

JUST PRETEND 117

Supplies: Cardstock (Bazzill); patterned papers (Paper Salon); chipboard letters (Me & My Big Ideas); die-cut letters, photo turns, photo corners (QuicKutz); die-cut scrolls template (Cosmo Cricket); page pebbles (Memories in the Making); brads (Creative Impressions); transparency (Grafix); chalk ink (Clearsnap); adhesive (Magic Scraps, Therm O Web, Xyron); Times New Roman font (Microsoft)

source guide

The following companies manufacture products featured in this book. Please check your local retailers to find these materials, or go to a company's Web site for the latest product. In addition, we have made every attempt to properly credit the items mentioned in this book. We apologize to any company that we have listed incorrectly, and we would appreciate hearing from you.

3L Corporation
(800) 828-3130
www.scrapbook-adhesives.com

3M
(800) 364-3577
www.3m.com

7 Gypsies
(877) 749-7797
www.sevengypsies.com

AccuCut
(800) 288-1670
www.accucut.com

Adorn It / Carolee's Creations
(435) 563-1100
www.adornit.com

All My Memories
(888) 553-1998
www.allmymemories.com

American Crafts
(801) 226-0747
www.americancrafts.com

American Hemp
(800) 469-4367
www.americanhemptwine.com

American Tag Company
(800) 223-3956
www.americantag.net

ANW Crestwood
(973) 406-5000
www.anwcrestwood.com

Arnold Grummer's
(800) 453-1485
www.arnoldgrummer.com

Artistic Wire, Ltd.
(630) 530-7567
www.artisticwire.com

Autumn Leaves
(800) 588-6707
www.autumnleaves.com

BasicGrey
(801) 544-1116
www.basicgrey.com

Bazzill Basics Paper
(480) 558-8557
www.bazzillbasics.com

Biblical Impressions
www.biblical.com

Chatterbox, Inc.
(888) 416-6260
www.chatterboxinc.com

Clearsnap, Inc.
(888) 448-4862
www.clearsnap.com

Collage Press
(435) 676-2039
www.collagepress.com

Cosmo Cricket
(800) 852-8810
www.cosmocricket.com

Crafter's Pick
(510) 526-7616
www.crafterspick.com

Crate Paper
(702) 966-0409
www.cratepaper.com

Creative Imaginations
(800) 942-6487
www.cigift.com

Creative Impressions
(719) 596-4860
www.creativeimpressions.com

Daisy D's Paper Company
(888) 601-8955
www.daisydspaper.com

DecoArt Inc.
(800) 367-3047
www.decoart.com

Dèjá Views
(800) 243-8419
www.dejaviews.com

Delta Creative
(800) 423-4135
www.deltacreative.com

Deluxe Designs
(480) 497-9005
www.deluxecuts.com

DMC Corp.
(973) 589-0606
www.dmc-usa.com

DMD Industries, Inc.
(800) 727-2727
www.dmdind.com

Doodlebug Design Inc.
(877) 800-9190
www.doodlebug.ws

EK Success, Ltd.
(800) 524-1349
www.eksuccess.com

Elan Patterns
(619) 442-1167
www.elanpatterns.com

Everlasting Keepsakes by faith
(816) 896-7037
www.everlastinkeepsakes.com

Fancy Pants Designs, LLC
(801) 779-3212
www.fancypantsdesigns.com

Fiber Scraps
(215) 230-4905
www.fiberscraps.com

Fiskars, Inc.
(866) 348-5661
www.fiskars.com

Font Garden
www.fontgarden.com

FontWerks
(604) 942-3105
www.fontwerks.com

gel·a·tins
(800) 393-2151
www.gelatinstamps.com

Go West Studios
(214) 227-0007
www.goweststudios.com

Grafix
(800) 447-2349
www.grafixarts.com

Heidi Grace Designs, Inc.
(866) 348-5661
www.heidigrace.com

Heidi Swapp/Advantus Corporation
(904) 482-0092
www.heidiswapp.com

Hero Arts Rubber Stamps, Inc.
(800) 822-4376
www.heroarts.com

Hillcreek Designs
(619) 562-5799
www.hillcreekdesigns.com

Ilford Imaging USA, Inc.
www.ilford.com

Imagination Project, Inc.
(888) 477-6532
www.imaginationproject.com

JewelCraft, LLC
(201) 223-0804
www.jewelcraft.biz

Junkitz
(732) 792-1108
www.junkitz.com

JustRite Stampers/Millenium Marking Company
(800) 545-7084
www.justritestampers.com

K & Company
(888) 244-2083
www.kandcompany.com

K&S Engineering
(773) 586-8503
www.ksmetals.com

Karen Foster Design
(801) 451-9779
www.karenfosterdesign.com

Keeping Memories Alive
(800) 419-4949
www.scrapbooks.com

Krylon
(800) 457-9566
www.krylon.com

Lacé
(800) 223-3956
www.americantag.net

Li'l Davis Designs
(480) 223-0080
www.lildavisdesigns.com

Ma Vinci's Reliquary
www.reliquary.cyberstamps.com

Magenta Rubber Stamps
(450) 922-5253
www.magentastyle.com

Magic Scraps
(904) 482-0092
www.magicscraps.com

MaisyMo Designs
(973) 907-7262
www.maisymo.com

Making Memories
(801) 294-0430
www.makingmemories.com

May Arts
(800) 442-3950
www.mayarts.com

Maya Road, LLC
(214) 488-3279
www.mayaroad.com

McCall Pattern Co., The
(800) 766-3619
www.mccall.com

McGill, Inc.
(800) 982-9884
www.mcgillinc.com

me & my BiG ideas
(949) 583-2065
www.meandmybigideas.com

Meadowbrooks Inventions, Inc.
(908) 766-0606
www.meadowbrookinventions.com

Melissa Frances/Heart & Home, Inc.
(888) 616-6166
www.melissafrances.com

Memories Complete, LLC
(866) 966-6365
www.memoriescomplete.com

Memories in the Making
(604) 850-8562
www.memoriesembellishments.com

Michaels Arts & Crafts
(800) 642-4235
www.michaels.com

Microsoft Corporation
www.microsoft.com

My Mind's Eye, Inc.
(866) 989-0320
www.mymindseye.com

Nature's Greetings - no source available

Nature's Pressed
(800) 850-2499
www.naturespressed.com

Norton
www.nortonabrasives.com

Pageframe Designs
(877) 553-7263
www.scrapbookframe.com

Panacea - no source available

Paper Adventures - see ANW Crestwood

Paper Salon
(800) 627-2648
www.papersalon.com

Pebbles Inc.
(801) 235-1520
www.pebblesinc.com

Petaloo
(800) 458-0350
www.petaloo.com

Pier 1
www.pier1.com

Plaid Enterprises, Inc.
(800) 842-4197
www.plaidonline.com

Polar Bear Press
(801) 451-7670
www.polarbearpress.com

Pressed Petals
(800) 748-4656
www.pressedpetals.com

Prima Marketing, Inc.
(909) 627-5532
www.primamarketinginc.com

Prism Papers
(866) 902-1002
www.prismpapers.com

Provo Craft
(800) 937-7686
www.provocraft.com

PSX Design
www.sierra-enterprises.com/psxmain

Queen & Co.
(858) 613-7858
www.queenandcompany.com

QuicKutz, Inc.
(888) 702-1146
www.quickutz.com

Ranger Industries, Inc.
(800) 244-2211
www.rangerink.com

Rose Art
(973) 535-1313

Rubba Dub Dub
(916) 391-2731
www.artsanctum.com

Rusty Pickle
(801) 746-1045
www.rustypickle.com

Sakura Hobby Craft
(310) 212-7878
www.sakuracraft.com

Sandylion Sticker Designs
(800) 387-4215
www.sandylion.com

Sassafras Lass
(801) 269-1331
www.sassafraslass.com

Scenic Route Paper Co.
(801) 225 5754
www.scenicroutepaper.com

ScrapArts
(503) 631-4893
www.scraparts.com

Scrappin' Extras
(403) 271-9649
www.scrappinextras.com

Scraptivity Scrapbooking, Inc.
(800) 393-2151
www.scraptivity.com

Scrapworks, LLC
(801) 363-1010
www.scrapworks.com

SEI, Inc.
(800) 333-3279
www.shopsei.com

Serendipity Designworks
(250) 743-7642
www.serendipitydesignworks.com

Sino Harvest Co., Ltd.
www.makinsclay.com

Stanley Hardware
(800) 622-4393
www.stanleyhardware.com

Stewart Superior Corporation
(800) 558-2875
www.stewartsuperior.com

Strathmore Papers
(also see Mohawk Paper Mills)
(800) 628-8816
www.strathmore.com

STYROFOAM
www.styrofoamcrafts.com

Sunshine Designs
(519) 762-6349
www.sunshinedesigns.ca

Sweetwater
(800) 359-3094
www.sweetwaterscrapbook.com

Ten Seconds Studio
www.tensecondsstudio.com

Textured Trios - no source available

Therm O Web, Inc.
(800) 323-0799
www.thermoweb.com

Tin Box Creations
www.tinboxcreations.com

Tsukineko, Inc.
(800) 769-6633
www.tsukineko.com

Two Peas in a Bucket
(888) 896-7327
www.twopeasinabucket.com

USArtQuest, Inc.
(517) 522-6225
www.usartquest.com

U.S. Shell, Inc.
(956) 554-4500
www.usshell.com

Venus Design Studio, LLC
(800) 221-6097
www.venusindustries.com

Walnut Hollow Farm, Inc.
(800) 950-5101
www.walnuthollow.com

We R Memory Keepers, Inc.
(801) 539-5000
www.weronthenet.com

Wimpole Street Creations
(800) 765-0504
www.wimpolestreet.com

Xyron
(800) 793-3523
www.xyron.com

Yarn Collection, The
(415) 383-9276
fibergoddess@msn.com

Zsiage, LLC
(718) 224-1976
www.zsiage.com

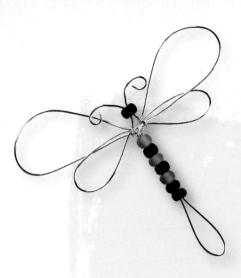

AS A MEMBER OF a creative family, Trudy's interest in art started at an early age and continued to grow throughout her school years and into college where she studied graphic and fine arts. But it wasn't until years later in November 2000 after she became an avid rubber stamper that Trudy first walked into a scrapbook store—and her new addiction for the art of scrapbooking began. Since being selected as one of the original Memory Makers Masters in 2003, she has become a regular artwork contributor to *Memory Makers* magazine and books. Her achievements include designing the cover art for the 2004 Layout Mania special issue and being featured in the October 2004 *Memory Makers* article appropriately titled "Truly Trudy." She also authored her first scrapbooking book titled *Embellished Emotions for Scrapbookers* in 2006.

After teaching and demonstrating for different manufacturers at U.S. and Canadian trade shows, Trudy has gained popularity amongst the teaching circuit and has taught at Camp Memory Makers for two years as well as on one of Memory Makers' Caribbean Croppin' Cruises. She can still be found teaching at scrapbook conventions and as a guest instructor at scrapbook stores in North America. Trudy and her artwork have also made numerous television appearances, and much of her work has been featured by *Memory Makers* founder Michele Gerbrandt on "Scrapbook Memories." In 2004, Trudy also made several guest appearances on the "DIY Scrapbooking" show with host Sandi Genovese.

Originally from England, Trudy now lives in Victoria on Vancouver Island in British Columbia, Canada, with her children and scrapbooking inspirations, Aysha and Alex, and their furry, four-legged companions, Tia and Moggie.

index

A

About the Author 126
Acrylics 16-18, 23, 37, 77, 79, 86, 95, 100, 112-113, 116
Adirondack Wash 49, 67, 80-83, 90-91
Air-Dry Clay 70-71
Albums 18, 22, 24, 38, 57, 69, 70, 87, 96, 112
Alcohol Inks 36, 76-77, 95, 116
All-about-me pages 13, 115
Animal pages 8, 15, 18, 22, 28, 30, 36, 43-45, 52, 57, 62, 76, 89, 97, 99, 109
Art Mediums, Chapter Four 64-83

B

Batik Resist Medium 80-81
Beads 15, 61, 106-107
Brads and Eyelets 14, 20, 24-25, 27, 32-36, 40, 44-45, 55-57, 61, 83-84, 90, 103, 109, 112-113
Burlap 46, 52-53, 55, 61
Buttons 10-11, 22-23, 38, 41, 45, 62, 78, 88, 100, 102, 113

C

Cardboard 98-99
Cards 11, 17, 24, 37, 48, 75, 83, 87, 99, 110, 115
Charms 15, 30, 35, 41-43, 49, 53, 55, 62, 64, 67, 83, 92
Chipboard 10, 12, 16-17, 23, 35-37, 42, 44, 54, 60-61, 67-69, 78, 82, 84, 88, 90, 92, 94, 96-97, 102-109, 113
Clear Elements, Chapter Six 104-117
Clipboards 102
Cork 54-55, 57
Crackle 64, 66-67

D

Distressing 10-11, 34-35, 38-39, 42, 55, 57, 62, 96, 98-99, 102-103
Dry Embossing 36-37, 39, 94-95, 104, 110

E

Embossing Metal 36-37, 39
Embroidery 20-21

F

Fabric 11-13, 19-24, 35, 38, 42, 46, 49, 53-55, 57, 62, 80-81, 83
Family pages 23, 25-26, 40, 46, 49, 53, 69, 71, 79, 94, 102, 106, 108, 112-114, 117
Fibers 15, 26-27
Flowers and Leaves 48-49
Frames 13, 54, 79, 113
Friendship pages 27, 32, 34, 63, 82, 106

G

Glass 14, 16-17, 100, 116-117
Glitter Glue 13, 16, 24-25, 43, 69, 71, 77, 79, 83, 86-87, 93, 95-96, 100, 109, 112, 115-116

H

Handmade Paper 48, 57, 84, 88-89
Hand Sewing 22-23
Hardware 18, 33-35
Hemp and Twill 10-11, 13, 22-23, 46, 49-50, 53, 55-58, 60-61, 66, 84, 88, 98-99, 103
Heritage pages 11, 39

I

Introduction 6-7

K

Kid pages 6, 10, 12-14, 16, 19, 31-32, 35, 41, 49-50, 54-55, 60, 64, 67, 74, 77, 80, 84, 88, 90, 98-101, 104, 109-110, 113, 116-117

L

Lace 8, 10-11, 13-15, 18, 24-25, 36, 57, 62, 69, 82, 84, 88, 103
Liquid Pearl 3, 13, 17-18, 25, 71, 104, 109, 113-114

M

Machine Sewing 6, 8, 10-19, 23, 26-28, 30-34, 37-39, 41-46, 49-50, 52-53, 55, 57, 61, 63-64, 67, 70-72, 74, 76-77, 80, 82, 84, 87-90, 98-99, 102, 104, 106, 108-111, 113-115, 117
Marauyma Mesh 62-63
Masks 46, 53, 69, 79,
Metals, Chapter Two 28-45
Metal Letters and Words 6, 11, 40-41, 92, 116
Metal Moldings 38-39, 43-44
Metal Tins 35, 83
Metallic Flakes 48, 78-79
Mica 48, 50-51
Mini books 18, 22, 24, 38, 57, 70, 87, 96, 112

N

Natural Elements, Chapter Three 47-63

P

Paper, Chapter Five 84-103
Paper Perfect 74-75
Paper Piercing 92-93
Patterned Paper 86-87
Puffy Paper 100-101

R

Rhinestones 24, 44, 65, 67, 83, 89, 96, 99, 110, 114
Ribbon 13, 15-17, 23-28, 30, 37, 44-45, 62-64, 67, 70-71, 74-76, 79, 82-83, 89, 92-94, 96, 103-104, 107, 110-114

S

Sandpaper 58-59
Sequins 22, 45, 108-109
Sewing Notions 10-11, 42, 61-62, 74
Shrink Plastic 114-115
Silk Flowers 13, 23-25, 27, 39, 43, 65, 67, 83, 95-96, 112, 114
Source Guide 124-125
Sports pages 31, 95
Step-by-step instructions 12, 14, 21, 26, 31-32, 37, 40, 45, 51, 54, 59, 66, 68, 73, 75-76, 79, 81, 91-92, 95-96, 101, 107, 112, 117
Supply Lists 118-123

T

Table of Contents 4-5
Tags 11, 33, 39, 49, 55, 57, 61-62, 102
Technique Tips 15, 25, 30, 32, 35, 43, 50, 53, 69, 86, 96, 99, 102, 107, 114
Textiles, Chapter One 8-27
Texture Paste 40, 68-69
Transfer Ink 72-73
Transparencies 25, 32, 51, 61-62, 66, 69, 72, 77, 80, 110-111, 117
Travel pages 20, 33, 36, 42, 44, 52, 57, 61, 66, 68, 72, 77-78, 80, 92-93, 100, 102-103, 110, 115, 117

W

Watercolor Paper 90-91
Wax Seals 27, 103
Wire 2, 28, 30-31
Wire Mesh 32-33, 35, 56, 64, 67
Wood 56-57

Get more inspiration from these Memory Makers Books!

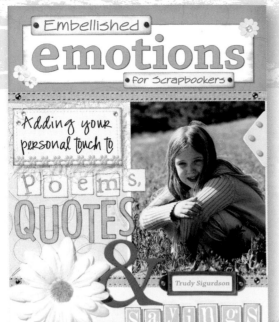

EMBELLISHED EMOTIONS FOR SCRAPBOOKERS

Learn from scrapbook artist Trudy Sigurdson on how to begin a journey into capturing emotion on scrapbook pages through the use of poems, quotes and sayings.

ISBN-13: 978-1-892127-84-6
ISBN-10: 1-892127-84-9

paperback
112 pages
Z0023

THE SCRAPBOOK DESIGNER'S WORKBOOK

Join author Kari Hansen as she takes the fear out of understanding and using design principles to create fabulous scrapbook layouts.

ISBN-13: 978-1-892127-95-2
ISBN-10: 1-892127-95-4

hardcover with enclosed spiral
128 pages
Z0533

TYPE CAST

Learn fresh, creative uses for a variety of type treatments as well expert tips on composing attention-getting titles and getting into the flow of journaling.

ISBN-13: 978-1-59963-003-8
ISBN-10: 1-59963-003-6

paperback
128 pages
Z0695

These books and other fine Memory Makers titles are available at your local scrapbook or craft store, bookstore or from online suppliers, including **www.memorymakersmagazine.com**.